Famous Writers
Non-Fiction Course

Famous Writers School
Westport, Connecticut

Famous Writers
Non-Fiction Course

Article and feature
writing

Volume IV

191-007A

The Famous Writers Courses are published with the
editorial advice and contributions of the
Guiding Faculty of the Famous Writers School

Faith Baldwin

John Caples

Bruce Catton

Bennett Cerf

Mignon G. Eberhart

Paul Engle

Bergen Evans

* Clifton Fadiman

Rudolf Flesch

Phyllis McGinley

J.D. Ratcliff

Rod Serling

Max Shulman

Red Smith

Mark Wiseman

Gordon Carroll, Director

Contents

Article and feature writing

Volume IV

Section V

Lesson ten

Editing and revising

Editing and revising copy doesn't become an editor's job until an accepted manuscript lies on his desk. But if the writer hasn't done some revising on his own, the editor won't likely buy his wares. So it's important that all writers practice the techniques of what the dictionary calls "preparing works for publication."

Revision is the first and most important step in this process. Earlier in this Course you were cautioned to "revise, revise, revise." Nothing is better for your copy, especially non-fiction, than reworking, editing and polishing.

To prove this and, at the same time, to show how a professional sweats over each line and page of copy, we're going to look over the shoulder of an article writer at work on his lead. The writer is William J. Lederer, whose book, *The Ugly American*, written with Eugene Burdick, has become a modern classic. The article was called "Miracle Under the Arctic Sea" and it appeared in the *Saturday Evening Post*. Then the *Reader's Digest* picked it up. Later it was expanded into a book, *The Last Cruise*.

Lederer composed 41 leads for this article and the process took him *three months*. Here are some of the leads he wrote, plus his critical comments on each, as he explains them in his book, *Spare-time Article Writing for Money:*

Lead No. 1

This lead tells the locale and the date—but that's about all. I decided the submarines would have to come closer to the beginning. The action, after all, revolved about the two submarines.

Four hundred miles north of the Arctic Circle, northwest of the northern tip of Norway, an angry gale raged down from the Polar regions. The mountainous waves and the roaring wind fought each other; as a wave lifted its great head into the air, sixty to a hundred feet above its own trough, the angry wind rushed in, knocking the gray wave top into a flash of icy-colored spray.

This was the Greenland Sea. August 25.

Although south of the ice pack, the spray and mist gave the air the iceberg-area look.

William J. Lederer composed 41 leads for his *Saturday Evening Post* article about a submarine cruise, "Miracle Under the Arctic Sea," before finally hitting upon one that satisfied him.

Underneath the turbulent surface, two American submarines, the *Cochino* and *Tusk,* tranquilly proceeded with tactical exercises.

Lead No. 2

The *Cochino* and *Tusk* were both "Guppies," submarines which, like giant eels, travel underwater at high speed. The Guppy must slither her way close to the victim before letting loose her explosives. Smooth-skinned, slippery, she can't bust or bruise her way into an advantageous position because she has no defense except camouflage and speed. To reach an attacking position the Guppy uses stealth; sneaking in low she runs between dangers.

Inside the 300-foot eel there twists a maze of propulsive equipment and torpedoes. The fact that men must live in the guts of this steel monster appears as an afterthought. First come the engines and the explosives; then, second fiddle, come the humans.

The submarines are at the beginning. But this lead reads like the beginning of a textbook. (There is no motion ahead in it: it is all essay.). Note I started with the author's point of view.

Lead No. 5

Before anyone can understand a story about the Submarine Navy, he must know how difficult it is to move about in these underseas boats, either topside or below. Almost every cubic inch inside their 300-foot length bulges with war equipment. The men—the brains which direct operations—have no places of their own; they eat in the after battery room, sleep wherever a bunk can be rigged, catch as catch can, surrounded by torpedoes, air compressors, manifolds, valves, and ballast tanks.

The submariner's seagoing existence consists of compression and crowding. It's "pull in your stomach, sailor, and squeeze to get to the messing table; it's flatten against the bulkhead so that your shipmate can reach his battle station; it's duck your head, brother, or you'll beat your brains out on the watertight doors." When in his bunk, a submarine sailor has no more room to wriggle in than he'll some day have in his coffin.

The lead remains static. It is descriptive, not narrative, and still reads like an essay. At this point I really didn't know what to do and was experimenting by throwing in every bit of information I could; with every new lead I tried changing information and rearranging it. No matter how wasteful this trial and error system appears, I believe it is the best way to find an effective lead. Actually, the trial and error method is not wasteful. The beginnings which are not used usually find a place somewhere else in the article.

Lead No. 8

At the end of August, the snorkels of two experimental submarines, the *USS Cochino* and *USS Tusk*, pushed their air-hungry snouts up through the surface of the Greenland Sea. The submarines ran submerged in one of the roughest and coldest oceans in the world. The Arctic Circle lay 400 miles to the south. The frozen wastes of Siberia bore south by east.

During the snorkeling exercises, the skippers permitted the junior officers to control the boats. The skippers relaxed. In the back of his mind Commander Rafael Benitez of the *Cochino* wrestled with a personal problem. How could he tell his Spanish-speaking father and mother—in Puerto Rico—about his new command? In Spanish, *cochino* has an obscene meaning. Perhaps they would not understand why such a name should be attached to a ship of the Navy.

At last I have a person in the lead, but still no forward action. The point of view has changed from the author's to that of Benitez.

Lead No. 12

No major change. I was still groping for a variation.

The two experimental submarines, *USS Cochino* and *USS Tusk,* surfaced in the center of the Greenland Sea. The warning weather broadcast, as the radioman put it, "was pretty damned accurate." Submerging again, using snorkels, they cruised leisurely south.

Running beneath a gale was old stuff now, and the skippers relaxed, permitting the junior officers to con. There wasn't even any shipping to worry about; the subs cruised in an isolated area outside the thousand-fathom curve, and 400 miles north of the Arctic Circle.

Supervising the *Cochino,* black-haired, serious, Rafael Benitez pondered a personal problem. How could he write his Spanish-speaking father and mother about his new command? In Spanish, *cochino* had an obscene meaning.

Lead No. 15

In lead 15 I wanted to see if perhaps the story would develop more easily from Philo's point of view. It didn't.

Mr. Robert Philo, the only civilian aboard the *USS Cochino,* sucked in his stomach and squeezed his way past valves, manifolds and switchboards to the after part of the boat. The equipment installed by his company lay back there; Martinez, the electrician's mate, had reported that the reading looked high.

Philo enjoyed his field trips in submarines; this one, in a new experimental-type boat, particularly thrilled him. He felt that he was a real part of the Navy; and that the delicate instruments he tested would help win the next war. The *Cochino* had been submerged in the Greenland Sea for three days now.

Lead No. 27

In lead 27, I began to make progress. I knew the story would have to start with Benitez's point of view, and that the problem of controlling the submarine should be within the first or second paragraph. I recognized that the scene of action would change so often that the reader would have a hard time knowing what time it was. Therefore, I decided to put in the hours from the ships' logs.

"From the patrol report of the *USS Tusk* and *USS Cochino:* 0004, 25 July. *USS Tusk* and *USS Cochino* engaged in routine cold-water operations in the Greenland Sea 400 miles north of the Arctic Circle, Latitude ——, Longitude——. Water temperature near freezing. Both boats running submerged a half-mile apart, communicating by sonar. Heavy seas overhead making it difficult for boats to maintain trim."

Beneath the surface of the Greenland Sea, the *USS Cochino* leaped and gyrated like a roller coaster out of control. The man on duty frantically varied ballast and adjusted hydroplanes, but the ship continued to broach. Commander Rafael Benitez checked the time. 0801. It would be a long day submerged. In these seas they couldn't even surface safely.

Lead No. 36

This lead was moving in the right direction. But on looking into my notes, I learned that Benitez was *not* in the Control Room at the time. He was above in the conning tower.

Commander Rafael Benitez watched the personnel on watch in the Control Room sweat as they tried to keep the submerged *Cochino* steady.

"Damn that storm!" he said.

At 0801 the *Cochino* wrenched violently, throwing Commander Benitez against the bulkhead. He saw the needle of the hydrogen indicator swing into the red danger sector. Almost simultaneously the general alarm clanged, announcing a state of emergency.

Lead No. 40 (next to last)

The skipper of the *USS Cochino,* Comdr. Rafael Benitez of Groton, Conn., was thrown against the conning-tower bulkhead. "Damn those . . . seas."

The ship wrenched violently. Benitez jumped up, went down the ladder to the Control Room.

"Get the battle-stations men on the controls!"

His experienced crew brought the boat to proper depth. The *Cochino* jolted again. Benitez saw the hydrogen indicator swing into the red danger position. He grabbed the microphone; all over the ship the warning came from the loudspeakers, "Hydrogen! Put out the Smoking Lamp." Sailors put out their cigarettes. A chief petty officer plunged the bowl of his pipe into a cup of coffee.

Before Benitez could issue another order, there was an explosion. The door of the Control Room opened. Men came through, yelling, "Fire!"

Lead 40 is dramatically sound; but it doesn't have sparkle. It needs polishing. The changes made are shown.

The moment this lead was on paper I felt that I had hit the right one. The approach had occurred to me several times previously, but hadn't quite jelled. Lead 40 sets the scene, starts the action, tells the reader that a submarine with people on it is in trouble, and establishes the point of view as being Benitez's.

	Line
The skipper of the USS *Cochino*, Comdr. Rafael	1
Benitez of Groton, Conn., ~~was thrown~~ *lost his balance and fell* against the	2
conning-tower bulkhead. *cc)* Damn those ... seas."	3
The ship ~~wrenched~~ *careened* violently. Benitez jumped up,	4
went down the ladder to the Control Room.	5
"Get the battle-stations men on the controls!"	6
His experienced crew ~~brought~~ *battled* the boat to proper	7
depth. The *Cochino* jolted again. Benitez *gasped as he)* saw the	8

hydrogen indicator swing into the red danger position.   9

He grabbed the microphone; all over the ship the *dreaded)*   10
(screamed
warning)~~came~~ from the loudspeakers, "Hydrogen! Put   11
frantically extinguished,
out the Smoking Lamp." Sailors ~~put out~~ /their   12

cigarettes. A chief petty officer plunged the bowl   13

of his pipe into a cup of coffee.   14
(a shock wave whipped through the Cochino and w
Before Benitez could issue another order, ~~there~~   15
a heavy thud pounded against the steel bulkhead
~~was an explosion.~~ The door of the Control Room opene~~d~~.   16
jostled)   *(banged)*
Men ~~came~~ through, yelling, "Fire!"   17

Line 2: "Was thrown" wasn't accurate. Benitez wasn't thrown like a ball. I substituted "lost his balance and fell" because that was what happened.

Line 4: "Wrench" was grammatically wrong, and didn't give the feeling of being out of control. "Careened" did.

Line 7: "Brought" was too tame. It didn't imply struggle, or give the impression of fighting the ship into submission. I used "battled" because I felt it was the right verb, and also it implied that the order given in the line above had been carried out.

Line 8: I inserted "gasped as he" to emphasize that something hazardous was happening.

Line 10: "Dreaded" inserted for same reason.

Line 11: "Came" is too static. It doesn't mean anything. This was an exciting announcement. The warning "screamed" from the speakers, and it couldn't have been any other word.

Line 12: "Put out" didn't paint the right picture. "Put out" gives the impression of slowly snuffing out a cigarette in some drawing-room ashtray. The fire in the cigarettes had to be eliminated with speed and finality. Not one tiny spark could remain in the tobacco. Therefore I used "frantically extinguished."

Line 16: "There was an explosion" is a simple statement of fact. Such writing does not excite the reader; he wants to learn about actions, and to deduce his own facts from them. Instead of "there was an explosion" I inserted "a shock wave whipped through the *Cochino* and with a heavy thud pounded against the steel bulkheads." Notice that instead of the one ineffective verb "was," we now have the active verbs "whipped" and "pounded." Also, the expression "a heavy thud pounded" brings in the element of noise. "Banged" was added to help produce the atmosphere of noise and temporary confusion.

Line 17: "Came" doesn't tell much. It is a tired, tame word. "Jostled" gives us a picture of what's happening.

This is the way the corrected version read:

The skipper of the *USS Cochino,* Comdr. Rafael Benitez of Groton, Conn., lost his balance and fell against the conning-tower bulkhead. "Damn those . . . seas."

The ship careened violently. Benitez jumped up, went down the ladder to the Control Room.

"Get the battle-stations men on the controls!"

His experienced crew battled the boat to proper depth. The *Cochino* jolted again. Benitez gasped as he saw the hydrogen indicator swing into the red danger position. He grabbed the microphone; all over the ship the dreaded warning screamed from the loudspeakers, "Hydrogen! Put out the Smoking Lamp." Sailors frantically extinguished their cigarettes. A chief petty officer plunged the bowl of his pipe into a cup of coffee.

Before Benitez could issue another order, a shock wave whipped through the *Cochino* and with a heavy thud pounded against the steel bulkheads. The door of the Control Room banged open. Men jostled through, yelling "Fire!"

When Lederer had finished the lead to his satisfaction, he could go rapidly into the sequence of narrative which, by now, was clear in his mind. Many other revisions—and a good deal of pen and pencil editing like that on the preceding pages—took place before he sent the piece to the *Post*. Its editors further shaped the copy before publication. When the piece was later expanded to book length, the author found it a far easier task than to melt down so many facts to magazine size.

The paste-over method of editing

This is a less common method than the use of pen or pencil, yet J.D. Ratcliff employs it with great success. He remarks:

It's a system that seems to work well for me. Anatole France used to revise and edit by pasting over. I don't think I derived it from him. It's probably original with many people. I used it on *Newsweek* when I was responsible for an enormous amount of copy. There simply wasn't time to rewrite, but if you had a bad paragraph you could take a razor blade and cut it out of the story, pasting on a new one. This technique grew for me into pasting right over the old copy.

By this pasting-over method I rearrange a whole story in sequential development. If I see there's something on page 7 that logically belongs on page 2, I simply cut it out and paste it there. It depends which is easier, in context, pasting over or cutting out and repasting. But either technique is useful.

In modern editing, paste has been replaced to some degree by transparent tape, which isn't as messy and has the advantage that you can see through it. This sample from "The Wonder of the Winds" shows how Ratcliff uses paste-over.

with India---Roman coins are still found there. But Egypt was
their main preoccupation---Rome had to have 20 million bushels of
Egyptian wheat a year to survive. Early along, observant Roman
                    in winter and spring
sailors noted that/there was a prevailing wind blowing up from
Egypt that would carry them across the Mediterranean in ~~as~~
~~little as~~ eight days. In summer ~~thisxxxxx~~ the wind reversed. They
did most of their hauling in spring.

We may think we live on earth. Actually we live in it---
at the bottom of a vast, turbulent, sea of air. At times this
                     was
sea above is is calm as a millpond. At others it moves with a
speed greater than ~~that of~~ a .45 bullet.

Ratcliff is one of the foremost non-fiction writers in America, yet he says he rewrites his original copy many times.

I doubt that a single word or sentence from an original draft ever ends up in the final draft precisely where it was. Or possibly not even from the second draft to the final draft. With the third rewriting you begin to come a little closer. You just go over and over it.

I think any successful writer must do this continuous revision. Editors tell me they're appalled at some of the things that come in. Sentences which aren't sentences, paragraphs which aren't paragraphs, and *non sequiturs*—right off there are two strikes against the article.

Editing on the typewriter

This third method is used in non-fiction by Bruce Catton. He likes to rewrite as he goes along, polishing and repolishing a sentence, xxxxxxxxx-ing out words, inserting sharper ones until each paragraph is the best he can do.

Since this method is so painstaking, we're including extended examples of it from Chapter Two of Catton's *Never Call Retreat*. By way of an explanatory note, Catton has reached the place in his narrative where he wants to describe the results of Lincoln's Emancipation Proclamation.

132

/

       The trouble was that emancipation came in with such a surprising rush. The
Proclamation had been an approach to the problem rather than a solution, and it had
been written by a man who supposed that once the government's intent had been stated
there would be time to make the delicate adjustments that were necessary. What was
happening in Missouri was a case in point; spurred by the President's warning, the
people of this slave state were trying to work out xxxxxx some arrangement that
would provide a slow transition, and the President was willing to allow a good deal
of margin for trial-and-error expedients in the hope that other slave states would
fall in line. But events were moving too fast. Emancipation was an accomplished
fact long before andone had done any planning, and the innumerable problems that
it brought were ////   and the greatest single change that ever took place in
the United States came in

       took place with

       suddenly it was something people were living with, even though no
one had had time to

Catton begins this segment as many professionals do—by simply
beginning. He knows that once under way, he'll keep going. And he does
so, for ten lines. Then he pauses and decides to revise.

132

2

The trouble was that events were moving too fast. The Emancipation Pro-

clamation had been nothing more than a statement of intent, written by a man who

supposed that there would be time to make the necessary adjustments. What was hap-

pening in Missouri was a case in point: the people of this slave state were trying

to work out a slow transition, and the President was willing to allow a margin for

trial-and-error expedients in the hope that other slave states would fall in line.

But emancipation came with a rush and there was x no time to adjust anything. The

greatest single change that ever took place in American life arrived with no ad-

vance planning at all. Men found that they were living with it while they were

still wondering whether it ought to happen at all.

In his notable speech Congressman Vallandigham kxd warned that nothing of
                          occur.
the kind could possibly kxppenxxbexdxxex The institution had too many roots and

the roots went too deep. Sudden change was out of the question.

"You cannot abolish slavery by the sword", he declared, "still less by

proclamations, though the President were to 'proclaim' every month. . . Neither,

sir, can you abolish slavery by argument. As well attempt to abolish marriage or

the relation of paternity."

This was a perfectly logical statement, robbed of its logic only by the
dismaying   xhxtxVxlixndighxmxxxitedxinpxssiblexxxxxxxtxxityxbxingxdxnx
xxkxxndxng fact that xixxxxyxxxxxbxingxxbxiixhxdxbyxthxxxxxxdxxndxbyxpxxxixmxtixmx
                      the impossible was actually being done.
Slavery was being abolished by the sword, and by proclamation; perhaps because
                                  by sudden fire and by uprising of the spirit,
there was no other way to do it,xx perhaps because in time of war imcomprehensible

things do happen.

Many writers would be content to carry on from the point
reached on the previous page. But Catton was dissatisfied, as is clearly
apparent in this second version of the passage.

132

3

The trouble was that events were moving too fast. The Emancipation Proclamation had been nothing more than a statement of intent, written by a man who supposed that there would be time to make the necessary adjustments. What was happening in Missouri was a case in point: the people of this slave state were trying to work out a slow transition, and the President was willing to allow a margin for trial-and-error expedients in the hope that other slave states would fall in line. But emancipation came with such a rush that there was no time to adjust anything. ~~The greatest single change that ever took place in American life arrived without benefit of advance planning.~~ Men found that they were living with it while they were still wondering whether it ought to happen at all.

In his notable speech Congressman Vallandigham warned that nothing of the kind could possibly occur. The institution had too many roots, and the roots went down too far in too many hearts. Sudden change was out of the question.

"You cannot abolish slavery by the sword; still less by proclamations, though the President were to 'proclaim' every month," he cried. "Neither, sir, can you abolisy slavery by argument. As well attempt to abolish marriage or the relation of paternity."

This was a perfectly logical statement, robbed of its logic by the dismaying fact that ~~the~~ what Vallandigham considered impossible was ~~actually being done~~. Slavery was being abolished by the sword and by proclamation, by fire and by sudden uprising of the spirit; perhaps because there was no other way to do it, perhaps because in time of war incomprehensible things do happen. And so the greatest single change that ever took place in American life arrived without the benefit of advance planning.

Here is a third version of the Catton typescript. Much of it is like the second, but he has made several subtle changes along the way.

5: *The Way of the Liberated*

The trouble was that events were moving too fast. The Emancipation Proclamation had been nothing more than a statement of intent, written by a man who supposed that there would be time to make all necessary adjustments. What was happening in Missouri was a case in point: the people of this state were trying to work out a slow transition, and the President was willing to allow a margin for trial-and-error expedients in the hope that other slave states would fall in line. But emancipation came with such a rush that there was no time to adjust anything. Men found that they were living with it while they still wondered whether it ought to happen at all.

In his notable speech Congressman Vallandigham warned that nothing of the kind could possibly occur. The institution had too many roots and the roots went down too far in too many hearts. Sudden change was out of the question.

"You cannot abolish slavery by the sword; still less by proclamations, though the President were to 'proclaim' every month," he cried. "Neither, sir, can you abolish slavery by argument. As well attempt to abolish marriage, or the relation of paternity."[1]

This was a perfectly logical argument, robbed of its meaning by the fact that what Vallandigham considered impossible was actually being done. Slavery *was* being abolished by the sword and by proclamation, by fire and by sudden uprising of the spirit; perhaps because there was no other earthly way to do it. The greatest single change in American life arrived without the benefit of any advance planning.

To begin with, the proclamation was taken with deadly seriousness by the people most concerned, the Negroes themselves. To others it might be no more than a piece of paper that would mean much or nothing depending on how the war went; to the Negroes it was the parting of the Red Sea. It meant freedom now and everywhere, as fast as the word could travel, and the Negroes acted on this belief. Even though it had always been buttressed by unlimited force, slavery in America really existed by the consent of the governed. This consent, to be sure, came largely because the governed were utterly helpless, but it was a basic element in the

Again, Catton made further changes before the printed page took shape. This is the final version, just as it appears in *Never Call Retreat*.

Some general views on editing

It doesn't matter which method of editing you use. Some writers use all three—pencil for word changes, paste-over for paragraphs, the typewriter for ideas which occur as you go along. The point is, don't ever think that because your piece is in typescript, there's something sacred about it. An article doesn't reach the "no more change" stage until the writer can't think of any significant way of improving it.

Red Smith, for example, likes to check his copy for clichés, lightly underlining each. He then attempts to replace them with better phrases. Being Red Smith, he usually succeeds. For example, he may have written this phrase:

Howard March, veteran coach of the Chicago Chiefs, can't determine what's wrong this season.

No matter what he writes about, a pro football game or a kids' marble tournament, Red Smith considers the cliché his natural enemy.

The phrase "veteran coach" is a cliché. Same with "can't determine." Smith marks both and on his second trip through the copy, he substitutes:

Howard March, resident Merlin of the Chicago Chiefs, can't make out what's wrong this season.

Being a sports writer and humorist, Smith has a style more flexible and colorful than that used in straight news writing, so the cliché in his natural enemy. Actually, Smith is so used to avoiding the cliché (and redundancy) that he would seldom write an original sentence like the first one above. More than likely, he'd edit and polish in his mind before trite words came to paper. This saves him valuable time in a business famous for pressing deadlines.

If Smith uses "resident Merlin" a couple of times (and if other writers swipe the phrase and overuse it), he must subsequently vary it. Perhaps "resident genie" will do next time in a similar context, or "master magician," or something along an entirely different tack. The point is, of course, that the cliché will come out and something fresher go in, as in the case of replacing "can't determine" with "can't make out." Both are fairly common, but the latter sounds better.

Eliminating words, phrases, sentences or even paragraphs isn't something you can make hard rules about. You have to say to yourself, as you reread your own prose: "Do I really need this word, this phrase, this sentence, this paragraph? Can this word be eliminated? Can this phrase be trimmed or bettered? Shouldn't this sentence be part of another? What would happen if I dropped this entire paragraph, or reduced it to a sentence?"

Honest answers almost always require change, by pencil, typewriter, scissors, paste or tape. But to do this professionally, you have to be painfully candid with yourself. The system of putting copy away for a few days—weeks if you can—and coming back to it cold, aids your perspective immeasurably, sharpens your pencil, probably shocks you into changes (which is all to the good), and focuses your writing in the light of impersonal reality.

Passive verbs and unproductive adjectives are easy to spot. Take this actual sentence from an industrial house organ:

It is to be hoped that all employees will take advantage of the company's recently-announced, generous, new forward-looking medical insurance health plan.

First, let's change the passive to active voice:

We hope that—or—The Company hopes that . . .

Now let's reduce the stream of adjectives at the end to:

. . . the company's (or your) generous new medical plan.

Better still:

. . . the company's new medical insurance plan.

It now reads in full:

We hope all employees will take advantage of the company's new medical insurance plan.

Why is the revised sentence better? Because if the medical plan is recently announced, it's obviously new and it's not up to the company to call it generous or forward-looking. Details will tell employees the story. They won't miss a word benefiting them. If it's called medical insurance, it patently concerns health. If it's as big a fringe benefit as implied, the word "generous" will be obvious to all who work there; no company horn-blowing will add to its merits.

If you have written: "Frank was told by his boss to try again," you can say it better: "The boss told Frank to try again."

If you've written: "Ed was congratulated by most of the group," this is a better way of saying it: "Most of the group congratulated Ed."

You may find you've written something like this: "The package was picked up, which she opened in great excitement"—a weak and confusing sentence. Try changing it to: "She picked up the package and opened it in great excitement." The second is a better sentence because it's active, not passive, and the modifiers are where they should be.

The technique of shortening sentences is a technique instinctively used by writers and editors from the moment they begin working on copy. To split one sentence of 40 words into two sentences of 20 words makes things easier and clearer for the reader. This is elemental revising.

Carrying this technique a step further, you may find too many choppy, short sentences in a row, and wish to combine a couple of them for change of pace and rhythm. Just as many consecutive long sentences weary the reader, so do many consecutive short sentences leave him breathless and irritated. He can't get going as he reads along. An occasional lapse into a longer, more flowing sentence pattern does wonders for style and reader interest.

The technique, reassembling parts of a piece and making inserts where these paragraphs or sentences fit better and make the meaning clearer, depends quite naturally on the context. No specific rules can be laid down. Non-fiction must flow from idea to idea, fact to fact, as though the writer had built the structure from the ground up and each new thought had precedent and preparation.

The importance of good transitions

Bridging, or transition, is the most difficult element of this flow-technique. If you're having trouble with bridges, reread the Lesson on good structure in Volume I of *Principles of Good Writing*. You'll recall word bridges like *besides, next, anyway, afterwards, finally, in short, then, for instance, therefore, nevertheless, furthermore, eventually,* etc.

There are, of course, many other transitional methods. In *Effective Writing*, H.J. Tichy points out a number of them in the following passage from *Silent Spring* by Rachel Carson:

From the green depths of the offshore Atlantic many paths lead back to the coast. They[a] are paths[b] followed by fish; although unseen and intangible, they are linked with the outflow of waters from the coastal rivers. For thousands upon thousands of years[c] the salmon[d] have known and followed these threads of fresh water that lead them back to the rivers, each returning to the tributary in which it spent the first months or years of life. So,[e] in the summer and fall of 1953,[f] the salmon[g] of the river called Miramichi on the coast of New Brunswick moved in from their feeding grounds in the far Atlantic and ascended their native river. In[h] the upper[i] reaches of the Miramichi, in the streams that gather together a network of shadowed brooks, the salmon[j] deposited their eggs that autumn[k] in beds of gravel over which the stream water flowed swift and cold. Such places,[l] the watersheds of the great coniferous forests of spruce and balsam, of hemlock and pine, provide the kind of spawning grounds that salmon must have in order to survive.

A fisherman nets salmon off the coast of New Brunswick.

(a) The pronoun *they* in the second sentence refers to *paths* in the first sentence. (b) The word *paths* occurs in the first and second sentences. (c) The time phrase *for thousands upon thousands of years* and the present perfect tense *have known* take the reader over a long span of time from the distant past to the present. (d) The specific word *salmon* echoes the general word *fish* of the preceding sentence. (e) The conjunction *so* prepares the reader for a similar act. (f) The time phrase *in the summer and fall of 1953* moves the reader from the span of time of sentence 3 to specific seasons in a specific year. (g) The word *salmon* echoes *salmon* in the preceding sentence and *fish* in the second sentence.

Sentences 3 and 4 are subtly parallel. In 3, "the salmon have known and followed these threads of fresh water that lead them back to the rivers, each returning to the tributary in which it spent the first months or years of life." In 4, "the salmon . . . moved in from their feeding grounds in the far Atlantic and ascended their native river." Such parallelism, with each sentence slightly different from the other, is modern. The older writers used more exact parallelism.

(h) The phrase *in the upper reaches of the Miramichi* places the reader. (i) The word *upper* subtly echoes the thought of *ascended* in the preceding sentence. (j) *Salmon* again; it connects with *salmon* in sentences 3 and 4 and *fish* in sentence 2; thus a main word runs through the paragraph. (k) The demonstrative *that* and the word *autumn* (echoing *fall* in the preceding sentence) connect the two sentences. But these connectives would come too late in sentence 5 if they were the only connectives between it and sentence 4. (l) *Such places,* the opening words of sentence 6, connect clearly with the closing words of sentence 5, *in beds of gravel over which the stream water flowed swift and cold.* Connecting the end of one sentence with the beginning of the next is a popular technique to achieve coherence.

Tracing the transitions in an editorial, a book or a well-written article will help a writer who wishes to improve the coherence of his writing. The techniques he observes in the writing of others will prove useful when he meets problems in revising his own writing to make it coherent. Good writing, like Rachel Carson's, illustrates for him the kinds of transitions and the number of transitions that are to be expected in modern paragraphs. More important to an advanced writer is the fact that good writing demonstrates the close and subtle linking of the sentences of a paragraph and the varied and interesting ways that words and phrases emphasize and strengthen that linking.

The same transitional methods used to link sentences within a paragraph are used to connect paragraphs. The best place for connections between paragraphs is early in the first sentence of a new paragraph. Transitions between paragraphs are usually stronger and more numerous than those between sentences, because a new paragraph begins a new idea, and the break between ideas is greater than the break between the related sentences of a paragraph.

Sometimes paragraphs are part of a larger pattern within an article or chapter, and transitions are easy. One paragraph may be the explanation of a general statement, and the next two paragraphs may be two examples. The connections in such a case are as easy to accomplish as in a single paragraph. But occasionally a marked break must be bridged, as for instance in moving a paragraph of generalization to another idea not closely related. And in a few cases, part of the thought development of a paper may be a stressing of the break in thought. Then, writers often use a sentence of transition or even a short paragraph.

Rachel Carson followed the paragraph just discussed with a brief one that repeats the idea of the preceding paragraph and adds in a sharply contrasting short sentence an important contrast in idea:

These events repeated a pattern that was age-old, a pattern that had made the Miramichi one of the finest salmon streams in North America. But that year the pattern was to be broken.

How smoothly this paragraph is connected by *these events* to the whole preceding paragraph. How well the *but* and the short sentence of foreshadowing prepare the reader for a complete change in action. These methods of developing a paragraph and of providing transitions are neither complex nor difficult. Therefore, the skillful ways in which an artist adapts them to his subject and his purpose are all the more fascinating and, I dare hope, inspiring.

The need for a detached eye

Whenever you write, you are tempted to use expressions of which you are fond and proud. Usually it will be just these words and phrases that will stop the reader or throw him off. You can't spot them while you are writing: you are too strongly attached to what has just sprung from your mind. But in the cold light of "the morning after," you should be able to look at them with a detached reader's eye.

The need for *transposing* may be harder to see. At first writing, we rarely hit on the best arrangement of words for emphasis. The rule is simple enough: the place for emphasis is *at the end*. But while we write we have a tendency to overlook the reader's need for sentence rhythm and build-up. Newspaper lead sentences, with their deliberate anticlimax, are fine material for anyone who wants to learn transposing.

VANCOUVER, Wash., March 24—Death instead of help came yesterday to all but two survivors of an Army plane crash in the mountains north of here despite their frantic attempts to signal search planes.

Hurriedly written newspaper stories, like the report of an Army plane crash, often lack proper emphasis.

Did you feel the emphasis on *help, two,* and *search planes*? It's almost impossible to get the meaning without rereading. Let's do a little transposing:

VANCOUVER, Wash., March 24—An Army plane crashed yesterday in the mountains north of here. The survivors tried frantically to signal search planes; but when help came, all but two had died.

Here is another example—a press-release lead:

An increase of nearly 50 percent in the reliance of American business on professional industrial designers to give their products consumer appeal from an art, engineering and merchandising standpoint was indicated in a survey by the American Management Association and the Society of Industrial Designers, released yesterday.

Transposed, this reads:

The American Management Association and the Society of Industrial Designers released a survey yesterday showing that American businessmen want to give their product consumer appeal from the standpoint of merchandising, engineering and art. Their use of professional industrial designers has increased 50 percent.

As we said, you will have done most of your revising when you cut your original copy to pieces and turn the sentences upside down. The rest of your morning-after work is hardly more than odds and ends.

There is punctuation, for one thing. As you shorten your sentences, you'll make commas into periods. Other commas you'll take out, since the better sentence rhythm will make them unnecessary. You can tie some of your short sentences together by using semicolons instead of periods—or colons, if the first sentence serves as a curtain raiser to the second.

You will improve the paragraphing—usually by breaking long paragraphs into two or three smaller ones. Your shorter sentences will force you into shorter paragraphs; there is a natural relation between the two.

Use punctuation for emphasis: underlining (for italics) words and phrases to be stressed, and putting parentheses around those you want to de-emphasize. You will help the rhythm of your sentences by using a dash here and there—like this.

A final thought on editing

Editing is often done not by the writer but by somebody else—the somebody else being the editor who buys your piece. At first, you may resent such outside editing. You may grumble to yourself: "I slave over my article (or book) until I'm satisfied that it says what I want it to say, in what I think is the best way to say it. Why should some stranger come along and stick his hand in?"

If your audience consisted of yourself, duplicated many thousands of times, professional editors would indeed be unnecessary. Your readers would like what you say, how you say it, and would understand *exactly* what you mean. But that's not the way it works out in real life. Any form of communication is imperfect, writing being more imperfect than some of the others.

What you put into a piece of writing and what a reader gets

out of it may be worlds apart. This is why an editor is often necessary. He acts as a go-between and makes sure, insofar as he can, that *his* readers will understand what *you* are really trying to say.

Rudolf Flesch on editing

I don't know whether efficiency experts have ever made time-and-motion studies of the work done by copy editors in a publishing house. If they have, they undoubtedly found that editors spend 90 percent of their time crossing out words in manuscripts and shifting around those that are left.

It's hard to remember this when you're your own editor, revising what you have written yourself. Let's face it: those words you liked so well when you wrote them will *probably* have to be reduced by half and completely rearranged.—Rudolf Flesch

Don't aim at posterity

Books have changed the course of history. Examples which spring to mind quickly are Tom Paine's *Common Sense* and Harriet Beecher Stowe's *Uncle Tom's Cabin*.

But to think of yourself as one who leaves footprints in the sands of time could be a grievous error. A writer requires perspective. He also requires a sense of humor—even the most serious of writers. If you have what you consider an important message to deliver to the world, by all means deliver it and do it as cogently and as persuasively as you can. But it is well to put posterity out of your mind.

If you want to think of yourself as a contributor to the welfare of the world, think of yourself as one who provides entertainment or food for thought, but not as a mover and shaper.—Max Shulman

Section VI

Lesson eleven

Writing about people

Alexander Pope said: "The proper study of mankind is man." He would have come closer to the truth if he'd said: "The *favorite* study of mankind is man."

In the entire area of non-fiction writing, by far the largest single part concerns people. To prove our point, let's analyze a recent issue of the *Reader's Digest*, a magazine that is extremely successful in pleasing a vast body of readers by furnishing a "mix" of articles. Breaking down articles under twelve headings, such as "Medicine," "Science," "Nature" and "People," we find that of 37 articles in the issue, 23 were about people.

What we're leading up to is this: your best subject to write about, particularly as a new writer, is *people*. For every article you might write on, say, philosophy, business or law, you can write and sell three on people. Editors are always looking for articles dealing with some facet of the activities of humanity.

You can write about people in many ways: about groups of people or about one particular person; you can write a story about what somebody did to overcome an obstacle; or a first-person article about how you got rid of termites in your basement. You can write a book about a subject without leaving the library (Miss Chute did it with *Shakespeare of London,* as we described in Lesson Four) or you can do an "as-told-to" article about an interesting personality who lives in your town, and do it all by interview.

Why are people so anxious to read about other people? The obvious reason, of course, is "identification." The reader compares himself with the central character of the article. Perhaps the piece is about a man who made a million dollars in the stock market in five years; the reader asks himself, "Why couldn't *I* do that?" Another piece might be about a woman who wrote a best seller, even though she was paralyzed and lived in a wheelchair. Again the reader puts himself in the woman's place, and marvels at her strength and determination in producing a whole book.

Another type of recognition is reverse-identification. An example might be, "The Four-Martini Lunch," an article describing how alcohol ruined a businessman's career. Here the reader says: "I'm too smart to do anything like that."

Of course, not all articles about people depend on identification. There may be no personal involvement at all; we might be interested in reading how an agricultural expert helped a group of farmers on the Isle of Arran to increase their crops. We would feel no sense of identification since Arran is remote from us and our experience. Yet we would still be interested.

It all boils down to this: nothing interests people like other people. Which would *you* rather read: an article about Mount Everest or about the men who *climbed* Mount Everest?

The subject of "Writing About People" is a vast one, but we can break it down into five viewpoints:

1. Personal adventure—the direct involvement of one or more people in an unusual train of events—exciting, comic or tragic.
2. People in the headlines.
3. People with interesting jobs or hobbies.
4. People who have achieved success.
5. People who have overcome handicaps.

Number one (personal adventure) can be either a first-person piece or a true story written about another person. The other four examples are mostly about other people. There are exceptions, of course, since the how-to-do-it magazines are full of first-person pieces about jobs and hobbies.

Now, let's look at each of these categories, seeking article ideas and techniques:

1. Personal adventure

You go back through your life and perhaps one dramatic, vivid experience stands out. You were on a railroad train with your father and mother. The train rammed a stalled engine in dense fog. For hours you lay trapped in torchlighted, twisted wreckage as rescuers worked feverishly and the locomotives burned eerily in the night. How a miracle of rain extinguished the fire and how wonderful it felt when you were finally freed from the wreckage gives you the basis for an exceptional personal adventure story.

Any dramatic experience—perhaps how you lay for hours trapped in the wreckage of a train—might make for a personal adventure article.

Or say you were Ethel, a younger child who always had to wear your sister Alice's hand-me-downs and whose birthday never seemed to be celebrated properly. One birthday, your parents gave you a party and you asked for a special cake with your name on it. At the triumphant moment the gorgeously lighted cake appeared, erroneously inscribed: "Happy Birthday, Alice." The painful memory of this episode, small as it was, can be turned into a short but poignant piece evoking high reader sympathy.

Or a memorable incident may have been funny and human, therefore worth retelling. Your husband's boss was supposed to arrive on a 5:30 commuting train. You were to pick up his car at the airport and drive to meet them at the station. But as you sat waiting for the train, a group of motorcycle police surrounded you, guns in hand.

It turned out you'd taken the wrong car at the airport. It was almost identical in appearance, color and license number to the boss's car. Both drivers had left their keys in the glove compartments. Thus, just as your husband and his boss arrived on the station platform, you found yourself a hunted "criminal," the center of more excitement than your town had known in months. How it happened—and how it was satisfactorily explained by your husband's boss—could make a fascinating, funny piece.

Personal experience may involve uncommon bravery in a blind child, a sick child, a lost child. It may be a story of resourcefulness or courage in one of your household pets. A national magazine published an unusual personal experience of a New England family faced with fire on Christmas Eve. Saved by a German shepherd puppy, they later found the dog dead on the second floor. It had gone back after a kitten, which the family discovered alive by the stairway, under the shelter of the shepherd's shaggy neck and crossed paws.

As we have said, personal adventure may also be someone else's. Adventurous people have been worth reading about since words were first put on paper. Retired now and living in your town is a famous flyer once lost for six weeks after a Pacific air crash. How he survived the terrible ordeal of tropic sun, exposure, thirst, hunger and fear is worth recounting, if you do it from a new angle.

One of the most harrowing of all personal adventure stories was the sinking of the *Titanic* on April 14-15, 1912, after she hit an iceberg in the North Atlantic. Hanson W. Baldwin, sensing the tremendous drama of the 660 saved and the 1,500 who went to their watery deaths, later recapped the arresting personal experiences in "R.M.S. Titanic" for *Harper's* magazine.

The article begins by describing the *Titanic*, largest ship the world had ever known, sailing from Southampton on her maiden voyage to New York on April 10. Advertised as "unsinkable" because her compartments theoretically could seal off any intake of sea water, the *Titanic* was also the fastest passenger ship ever built and was out to break the transatlantic speed record on her first trip.

Aboard were more than 2,000 souls, many of them people of great importance in the industrial, journalistic, social and artistic worlds of the time. Col. John Jacob Astor was bringing his young bride home. The vice president of the Pennsylvania Railroad and the president of the Grand Trunk Railroad of Canada were passengers. Major Archibald Butt, military aide to President Taft, was proud to be on such a distinguished passenger list, which also included Francis D. Millet, the painter; Mr. and Mrs. Isidor Straus, of the banking and merchant family; J. Bruce Ismay, chairman and managing director of the White Star Line, who had unlimited faith in his "unsinkable" floating palace; and dozens of other celebrities from all walks of life on both sides of the Atlantic.

Disregarding constant warnings of icebergs ahead, the *Titanic's* officers plunged her at record speed through the dark seas. Murdoch, her First Officer, and Lightoller, her Second Officer, kept smelling disaster, yet were under orders to proceed full steam ahead. Bride, the Second Wireless Operator, and Phillips, First Operator, stayed near their vital posts as though sensing trouble.

Notice how you, while reading this article, put yourself in the place of those you're reading about—a true test of personal adventure non-fiction. When the following paragraphs appear in Mr. Baldwin's article, the *Titanic* has just struck an iceberg. A 300-foot gash has been ripped in her bottom and icy water pours into the watertight compartments which the ship's designers had boasted were impenetrable. The piece continues:

The sinking of the *Titanic*, shown here in an artist's drawing, is one of the most harrowing of all personal adventure stories.

Use of the narrative method is effective, especially the occasional time breaks. You feel the ship sinking as you read, aware of the terrible personal experience these men and women are enduring.

At 12:20 the water burst into the seamen's quarters through a collapsed fore and aft wooden bulkhead. Pumps strained in the engine-rooms—men and machinery making a futile fight against the sea. Steadily the water rose.

The boats were swung out—slowly; for the deckhands were late in reaching their stations, there had been no boat drill, and many of the crew did not know to what boats they were assigned. Orders were shouted; the safety valves had lifted, and steam was blowing off in a great rushing roar. In the chart house Fourth Officer Boxhall bent above a chart working rapidly with pencil and dividers.

12:25 A.M. Boxhall's position is sent out to a fleet of vessels: "Come at once; we have struck a berg."

To the Cunarder *Carpathia* (Arthur Henry Rostron, Master, New York to Liverpool, 58 miles away): "It's a CQD, old man. Position 41–46N; 50–14W."

The blue wireless spark danced: "Sinking; cannot hear for noise of steam."

12:30 A.M. The word is passed: "Women and children in the boats."

Stewards finish waking their passengers below; life-preservers are tied on; some men smile at the precaution. "The *Titanic* is unsinkable." The *Mt. Temple* starts for the *Titanic;* the *Carpathia,* with a double watch in her stokeholds, radios, "Coming hard." The CQD changes the course of many ships—but not of one; the operator of the *Californian,* nearby, has just put down his earphones and turned in.

The CQD flashes over land and sea from Cape Race to New York; newspaper city rooms leap to life and presses whir.

On the *Titanic,* water creeps over the bulkhead between No. 5 and 6 firerooms. She is going down by the head; the engineers—fighting a losing battle—are forced back foot by foot by the rising water. Down the promenade deck, Happy Jock Hume, the bandsman, runs with his instrument.

12:45 A.M. Murdoch, in charge on the starboard side, eyes tragic, but calm and cool, orders boat No. 7 lowered. The women hang back; they want no boat ride on an ice-strewn sea; the *Titanic* is unsinkable. The men encourage them, explain that this is just a precautionary measure: "We'll see you again at breakfast." There is little confusion; passengers stream slowly to the boat deck. In the steerage the immigrants chatter excitedly.

A sudden sharp hiss—a streaked flare against the night; Boxhall sends a rocket toward the sky. It explodes, and a parachute of white stars lights up the icy sea. "God! Rockets!" The band plays ragtime.

No. 8 is lowered, and No. 5. Ismay, still in dressing gown, calls for women and children, handles lines, stumbles in the way of an officer, is told to "get the hell out of here!" Third Officer Pitman takes charge of No. 5; as he swings into the boat Murdoch grasps his hand. "Goodby and good luck, old man."

No. 6 goes over the side. There are only twenty-eight people in a lifeboat with a capacity of sixty-five.

A light stabs from the bridge; Boxhall is calling in Morse flashes, again and again, to a strange ship stopped in the ice jam five to ten miles away. Another rocket drops its shower of sparks above the ice-strewn sea and the dying ship.

1:00 A.M. Slowly the water creeps higher; the fore ports of the

Written long before the television show "Dragnet" came into being, this article employs the familiar periodic time device so telling in suspenseful narration.

The drama of the operator on the *Californian* who has just laid down his earphones and turned in for the night—minutes before the *Titanic's* first distress signal. And the *Californian* might have saved so many—poignancy typical of personal adventure pieces.

Use of quotations from passengers and crew gives authenticity to the tale. This is good non-fiction narrative technique.

Use of present tense heightens the suspense. It is a good device, for the minutes tick away and the reader knows the ship is sinking with each passing second. The reader's sympathy goes more and more to those left aboard, and their dreadful personal experience, now beautifully retold.

Titanic are dipping into the sea. Rope squeaks through blocks; lifeboats drop jerkily seaward. Through the shouting on the decks comes the sound of the band playing ragtime.

The "Millionaires' Special" leaves the ship—boat No. 1, with a capacity of forty people, carries only Sir Cosmo and Lady Duff Gordon and ten others. Aft, the frightened immigrants mill and jostle and rush for a boat. An officer's fist flies out; three shots are fired in the air, and the panic is quelled . . . Four Chinese sneak unseen into a boat and hide in its bottom.

1:20 A.M. Water is coming into No. 4 boiler room. Stokers slice and shovel as water laps about their ankles—steam for the dynamos, steam for the dancing spark! As the water rises, great ash hoes rake the flaming coals from the furnaces. Safety valves open; the stokers retreat aft, and the watertight doors clang shut behind them.

The rockets fling their splendor toward the stars. The boats are more heavily loaded now, for the passengers know the *Titanic* is sinking. Women cling and sob. The great screws aft are rising clear of the sea. Half-filled boats are ordered to come alongside the cargo ports and take on more passengers, but the ports are never opened— and the boats are never filled. Others pull for the steamer's light miles away but never reach it; the lights disappear, the unknown ship steams off.

The water rises and the band plays ragtime.

1:30 A.M. Lightoller is getting the port boats off; Murdoch the starboard. As one boat is lowered into the sea a boat officer fires his gun along the ship's side to stop a rush from the lower decks. A woman tries to take her Great Dane into a boat with her; she is refused and steps out of the boat to die with her dog. Millet's "little smile which played on his lips all through the voyage" plays no more; his lips are grim, but he waves good-by and brings wraps for the women.

Benjamin Guggenheim, in evening clothes, smiles and says, "We've dressed up in our best and are prepared to go down like gentlemen."

1:40 A.M. Boat 14 is clear, then 13, 16, 15 and C. The lights still shine, but the *Baltic* hears the blue spark say, "Engine-room getting flooded."

The *Olympic* signals, "Am lighting up all possible boilers as fast as can."

Major Butt helps women into the last boat and waves good-by to them. Mrs. Straus puts her foot on the gunwale of a lifeboat, then she draws back and goes to her husband: "We have been together many years; where you go I will go." Colonel John Jacob Astor puts his young wife in a lifeboat, steps back, taps cigarette on fingernail: "Good-by, dearie; I'll join you later."

1:45 A.M. The foredeck is under water, the fo'c'sle head almost awash; the great stern is lifted high toward the bright stars; and still

[margin note 1:] Juxtaposition of the nearly empty lifeboat and its Lord and Lady passengers with the frightened immigrants. The four Chinese who sneak unseen into a boat and hide there point up the tremendous variety of the passenger list of the world's greatest ship. Again, a steamer's light (presumably the *Californian,* which never heard the distress call) is moving away from the lifeboats in the ice-strewn North Atlantic.

[margin note 2:] Of all the personal experiences and reactions in this dramatic story, none is more heartwarming or telling than Mrs. Straus's refusal to get into a lifeboat without her husband.

the band plays. Mr. and Mrs. Harris approach a lifeboat arm in arm.

Officer: "Ladies first, please."

Harris bows, steps back: "Of course, certainly; ladies first."

Boxhall fires the last rocket, then leaves in charge of boat No. 2.

2:00 A.M. She is dying now; her bow goes deeper, her stern higher. But there must be steam. Below in the stokeholds the sweaty firemen keep steam up for the flaring lights and the dancing spark. The glowing coals slide and tumble over the slanted grate bars; the sea pounds behind that yielding bulkhead. But the spark dances on.

The *Asian* hears Phillips try the new signal—SOS.

Boat No. 4 has left now; boat D leaves ten minutes later. Jacques Futrelle clasps his wife: "For God's sake, go! It's your last chance; go!" Madame Futrelle is half-forced into the boat. It clears the side.

There are about 660 people in the boats, and 1,500 still on the sinking *Titanic*.

On top of the officers' quarters men work frantically to get the two collapsibles stowed there over the side. Water is over the forward part of A deck now; it surges up the companionways toward the boat deck. In the radio shack, Bride has slipped a coat and lifejacket about Phillips as the First Operator sits hunched over his key, sending—still sending—"41—46N; 50—14W. CQD—CQD—SOS—SOS."

The Captain's tired white face appears at the radio-room door: "Men, you have done your full duty. You can do no more. Now, it's every man for himself." The Captain disappears—back to his sinking bridge, where Painter, his personal steward, stands quietly waiting for orders. The spark dances on. Bride turns his back and goes into the inner cabin. As he does so, a stoker grimed with coal, mad with fear, steals into the shack and reaches for the lifejacket on Phillips' back. Bride wheels about and brains him with a wrench.

2:10 A.M. Below decks the steam is still holding, though the pressure is falling—rapidly. In the gymnasium on the boat deck the athletic instructor watches quietly as two gentlemen ride the bicycles and another swings casually at the punching bag. Mail clerks stagger up the boat deck stairways, dragging soaked mail sacks. The spark still dances. The band still plays—but not ragtime:

Nearer my God to Thee,
Nearer to Thee . . .

A few men take up the refrain; others kneel on the slanting decks to pray. Many run and scramble aft, where hundreds are clinging above silent screws on the great uptilted stern. The spark still dances and the lights still flare; the engineers are on the job. The hymn comes to its close. Bandmaster Hartley, Yorkshireman violinist, taps his bow against a bulkhead, calls for "Autumn" as the water curls about his feet, and the eight musicians brace themselves against the ship's slant. People are leaping from the decks into the nearby water—the icy water. A woman cries, "Oh, save me!" A man answers, "Good

In the Edwardian world of the *Titanic,* it's most natural for Mr. Harris to step back and say, "Of course, certainly; ladies first." The tragedy of the *Titanic* is in part the self-assurance of "society" in an "unsinkable ship." It is the end of an era, a very telling factor in this adventure piece.

In many ways, the story of the coal stoker, mad with fear, trying to steal the radioman's lifejacket is the most dramatic scene in this whole fantastic biography of death.

Incredible as it must seem to the reader, the reported fact that two gentlemen are riding bicycles in the gymnasium and another punches a bag somehow dramatizes the incredible aura in which the *Titanic* disaster happened.

The periodic phrase: "The spark still dances" tells of the heroism of Phillips, at his post to death, though officially relieved by the Captain. The fact that the band is still playing, not ragtime now but "Nearer my God to Thee," is touching in the extreme.

lady, only God can save you now." The band plays "Autumn":

God of mercy and compassion!
Look with pity on my pain . . .

The water creeps over the bridge where the *Titanic's* master stands: heavily he steps out to meet it.

2:17 A.M. Men run about blackened decks; leap into the night; are swept into the sea, by the curling wave which licks up the *Titanic's* length. Lightoller does not leave the ship; the ship leaves him; there are hundreds like him, but only a few who live to tell of it. The funnels still swim above the water, but the ship is climbing into the perpendicular; the bridge is under and most of the foremast; the great stern rises like a squat leviathan. Men swim away from the sinking ship; others drop from the stern.

The band plays in the darkness, the water lapping upwards:

Hold me up in mighty waters
Keep my eyes on things above,
Righteousness, divine atonement,
Peace and everlas . . .

The forward funnel snaps and crashes into the sea; its steel tons hammer out of existence swimmers struggling in the freezing water. Streams of sparks, of smoke and steam, burst from the after funnels. The ship upends to 50 to 60 degrees.

Down in the black abyss of the stokeholds, of the engine-rooms, where the dynamos have whirred at long last to a stop, the stokers and the engineers are reeling against hot metal, the rising waters clutching at their knees. The boilers, the engine cylinders, rip from their plates; crash through bulkheads; rumble—steel against steel.

The *Titanic* stands on end, poised briefly for the plunge. Slowly she slides to her grave—slowly at first, and then more quickly—quickly, quickly.

2:20 A.M. The greatest ship in the world has sunk. From the calm, dark waters, where the floating lifeboats move, there goes up, in the white wake of passing, "one long continuous moan."

Years later, Walter B. Lord wrote his best seller, *A Night to Remember,* extending the drama to a full-length work. The story of the *Titanic* had been told many times; yet when all the angles, all the eyewitness accounts, all the small tragedies were placed between the covers of a single book, the accumulated detail was staggering—and the account was fascinating.

Any vivid personal experience makes memorable reading, and few can match the terrors of the *Titanic's* last hours. It doesn't have to be your own adventure to be salable. Almost

The tremendous size of the great ship, its power to sweep humans down with it, its final upending agony, are factors in a great personal drama, told to perfection in present tense, chronologically.

The author's enormous accumulation of details, painting the scene so no reader can forget it, proves the value of facts to non-fiction.

Few personal experience articles can top Mr. Baldwin's.

any editorial market will be eager to see your manuscript if it's really exciting.

2. People in the headlines

Feature writing about people in the limelight involves the whim of fate, the freakishness of circumstance which catapults some men and women into a national spotlight. They always offer feature article possibilities when a peculiar casting of the dice involves your own area. It's surprising how often this happens—if you'll only watch for it.

In a typical town in the course of a year, the following situations may well arise from which you can harvest a good article about people in the headlines:

1. A local hero, often a most unusual case and one well worth reading about in any region of the country.
2. A movie or television star arrives for a vacation or to visit a relative.
3. A local luncheon club brings in a prominent industrialist at a newsworthy moment.
4. A local man is elected to state office.
5. A child has her Christmas tree months in advance because she'll die of leukemia by autumn.

The idea's the same in any case. A local person might run into a highly exciting or humorous adventure. You could sell a story on such a subject to a local publication, but a national magazine probably wouldn't take it because of the person's lack of glamor. But let that same adventure happen to someone in the headlines and you have a chance of selling it to one of the big magazines.

There's an element of "scale" here: something exciting happens to a local person and you've got a local sale; the same adventure happens to a leading personality and you're trying for the Big Leagues. However, if something really unusual and exciting happens to a local person, the adventure itself may get you and your story on the cover of a mass magazine.

3. People with interesting jobs or hobbies

Here's a beginning list of unusual occupations to give any writer a start on an article idea for a national magazine:

1. A co-ed extracts medicinal venom from poisonous snakes to pay for her education.
2. A small-town surgeon collects rare dueling pistols, including the one with which Burr shot Hamilton.

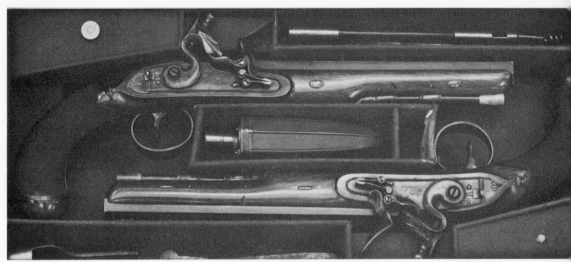

People with unusual hobbies—a small-town surgeon who collects rare dueling pistols—are always good article possibilities.

3. A man makes a success of a museum devoted to music boxes and other mechanical instruments.
4. A girl X-ray technician tests new parachutes as a sideline.
5. A professional executioner for five States has no friends.
6. A Methodist minister becomes a national golfing champion, but never plays on Sunday.
7. A man retires at 65 after a lifetime repairing high-tension wires.
8. A mechanic makes his living repairing and reconditioning Stanley Steamer automobiles.
9. A woman makes a fortune out of inventing practical jokes, tricks and April Fool gadgets.
10. A one-legged man gives exhibitions of fancy skiing.
11. A fireman turns his gardening hobby into a profitable nursery business.
12. A nature-loving nurse runs a sanctuary for waterfowl.

You can find similar ideas in your own backyard if you'll only look. Articles on interesting jobs and hobbies are sure to get readership when they're out of the ordinary and well written.

4. People who have achieved success

In *Modern Feature Writing,* DeWitt C. Reddick says that most individuals daydream of the kind of person they would like to be and the success they'd like to achieve. He tells how editors recognize this trait in readers:

They have a feeling of kinship with those who have gained that success; from stories about such people they gain courage, inspiration and often bits of practical guidance. Newspaper and magazine editors, recognizing this universal yearning for success, make a place for articles on men and women who have risen in their field of work.

But success stories have an appeal for general magazines only when the central figure is nationally known or when his business has unique distinction. Leading magazines, for instance, carried many articles on a man who achieved success and fortune by showing how you could win friends and influence people, largely through the way you speak. The *American Magazine* was famous for two generations for its Horatio Alger and Cinderella success stories. Less successful readers were moved deeply by these stories, gaining courage, inspiration and practical guidance. If someone else could do it, so could they in our rags-to-riches America.

5. People who have overcome handicaps

Most of us support the underdog in any fight. We are stirred by the man or woman who fights against a handicap and overcomes it. The handicap may be physical, it may be a personality weakness, it may be financial. It may involve religion, race or color. Whatever the problem, most readers feel sympathy for the handicapped.

A blind girl goes on a national television show and brings down the house as a violinist. Immediately she becomes article material.

An eminently successful man tells how he conquered an uncontrollable temper. His story is a natural in the category of personal experience.

In boyhood, a well-known TV performer had one leg crippled by polio. By sheer determination he exercised it to the point that he now walks normally—and even tap dances.

A 36-year-old mother raises six children by driving a truck

at night between Detroit and Chicago, and yet, there's not a delinquent in the household.

The interesting person may be yourself or someone you know well. The interest may not lie precisely in the person but in something that person has done. Since man during the ages has consistently sought better things through self-improvement, articles blossom from this trait as from no other in the whole field of non-fiction.

The odd and the strange

Another important ingredient of non-fiction is the odd or the strange. Look at these provocative titles, selected from national magazines:

"Why Some Women Reject Their Babies"
"Conquest of Death Before Birth"
"She Didn't Speak for Forty Years"
"How to Avoid Work"
"The Women Who Wait"
"Washington Wasn't Our First President"

Unusual objects, events, customs—the strange or odd in any context—contain inherent reader interest. Look again at the list of titles above. Every one is offbeat and every one involves personal experience—or its how-to-do-it, art-of-living relative. If any of the articles lacked the element of oddity or the fascination all readers have with self and personal experience, they would fail. But each has both ingredients to a remarkable degree and is therefore a highly salable idea.

Take the first title. *Reject* is the key word. Since mother-love is regarded as one of the basic human instincts, the thought of a woman rejecting her baby comes as a shock. The urge to read is tremendous.

The pull of the next title is in the seeming impossibility of conquering death before life has begun. An alternate title, "Saving Lives of Babies in the Womb," while equally accurate and effective in itself, has nowhere near the stopping power.

Why didn't the woman speak for forty years? How did she manage to get along without speaking? Self-identification is as much a part of odd personal experience as it is of other non-fiction articles.

The fourth title gets its punch from the word *avoid*. We all want to avoid work when we can; but for a publication to come out and teach us how to do it—this will stop anybody.

"The Women Who Wait" is an ominous title to begin with, but the burden of the threat lies behind *wait*. What are they waiting for? If the title were "Women Who Await Word from Their Husbands in the Army," it would tell the same story, and do it more fully; but the very incompleteness of "The Women Who Wait" adds to the feeling of suspense.

The fact that George Washington wasn't our first President is probably news to most people and, of course, it's a trick. We had other Presidents who were presiding officers of our government during the Articles of Confederation, prior to the Constitutional Convention. The trick, however, does make us read, and although the piece doesn't mislead the reader, it entertains and enlightens him through biographical non-fiction.

Other personal experience techniques

Many articles win readers without a catchy title and lead. Music or literary criticisms, for example, don't need them. Nor do certain philosophical pieces, or articles about history or controversies in which the issue is well known. And technical non-fiction is read within a profession or trade, regardless of headline. But in such cases, the reader knows the subject and so knows in advance that he's going to be interested.

The personal experience article, however, is almost always a one-shot. It has no precedent and no continuing readership. The reader has no preconceived ideas about it. Hence, the need for setting a trap to catch his attention.

After the title has grasped the reader's attention, you must have a smart lead to get him started reading the piece itself. How do you go about finding your best lead? Every article has its own beginning, its dramatic highlight. This one big fact or idea is the theme around which you'll build your story (and the title) and from which you'll fashion a provocative lead.

You begin by asking yourself a few questions about the theme. Is it a departure from the familiar? Is it controversial? Is it new—newsy in the sense that the reading public has never heard of it before? Then you're on the track of true reading bait. Is it possible to pull the drama into focus? If not, discard the lesser ideas and dramatize the best lead.

Let's look at lead possibilities that a writer assembled in the course of planning a feature article on amateur painting. He is amazed at how many people now paint for recreation and how well they do it. He has sensed a trend and by now has ten possible themes for a feature lead. These are:

1. Tremendous rise in amateur painting.
2. Grandma Moses' success gave it momentum.
3. Churchill, Eisenhower helped amateur painting.
4. Artists' supplies up 400 percent in last five years.
5. Paralyzed artist paints with his teeth.
6. Over 10,000,000 Americans paint for fun.
7. Fastest-growing hobby among older people.
8. Some have become famous as artists.
9. Many have gone from former jobs to art jobs.
10. Longer life span and retirement are factors.

The writer looks down the list and checks a few numbers. Many of the statements are interesting; all are pertinent to the article since they tend to prove his point or theme. But only two or three have the special dramatic quality that writers seek for feature leads. Let's evaluate them one at a time.

The first statement is general and unproved, though interesting. It will draw readership but not by itself. It has to be woven into the fabric or it won't stand up. There may well be a tremendous rise in amateur painting, but the author must justify the statement with facts and statistics.

Grandma Moses did give amateur painting a shot in the arm. But that was years ago. It isn't newsworthy now. Neither is the fact that Eisenhower and Churchill used to paint for recreation. Readers won't be hooked with this sort of stale bait, though the facts are useful somewhere.

But No. 4 is a statistic. It isn't guessing—it's fact. No. 5 is highly dramatic and by far the best bet for a title and a lead. No. 6 supports the thesis with another startling statistic, though it isn't the entire lead itself. No. 7 is a stronger statement than No. 1, because No. 7 is specific, not general—"fastest-growing hobby among older people" persuades the reader to accept the writer's premises, since there are far more older people today than there used to be, which ties in with No. 10. No. 8 and No. 9 are supporting facts, but not as dramatic as No. 5.

So our non-fiction writer rightly decides to call the piece: "He Paints with His Teeth." This isn't the biggest fact, but it's the most intriguing. The author knows that the artist's arms are paralyzed, but he doesn't have to say so in the title. It's implied—a dramatic fact pertinent to the whole theme. Imagine holding a brush in your teeth and leaning toward the easel to put in a delicate shadow, without help of any sort!

The writer then fashions a lead something like this:

Albert Ford of Alhambra, California, lost the use of both arms in a paralyzing illness five years ago, but you'd never know it to look at the watercolors which have made this 66-year-old man famous. He painted them by holding the brush in his teeth and if you don't think that's quite a stunt, try it.

The rising popularity of amateur painting might make for an interesting personal experience article.

Albert Ford's remarkable story is but one of many in America's fastest-growing pastime, amateur painting. Over 10,000,000 Americans now paint for fun. Increased leisure time, longer life span, retirement at an early age—all are factors in the amazing art boom.

The sale of painting supplies is up 400 percent over five years ago. Some amateurs have gone on to become professional illustrators and artists. But, in general, the growing hobby is just that—a pleasant means of passing the time with no reward except the sense of fulfillment and relaxation which led Churchill and Eisenhower to enjoy painting.

You might have started an article on amateur painting in dozens of ways, but by beginning with the man who paints with his teeth, you've hooked the reader. Suppose you had begun this way:

The tremendous rise in amateur painting has upped the sale of paint supplies 400 percent in the last five years and by now more than 10,000,000 Americans paint for fun.

What you've written is factual enough, but not as dramatic as Albert Ford's story. Besides, what sort of title could you put on this? You might choose one of these:

"Painting Supplies Up 400 Percent"
"Ten Million Americans Paint for Fun"
"The Rise of Amateur Painting"

Legitimate—but dull. Nowhere near as alluring as: "He Paints with His Teeth."

Why should this be so? We have to go back to a premise of this Lesson—that personal experience is a powerful force for readership because of identification with self. Few readers can identify with a statistic. But all of them can mentally put themselves in the place of a paralyzed man who has overcome an appalling handicap. The reader glows in this victory against odds and is lured into reading on. By dramatizing Albert Ford's remarkable experience, our writer has turned dull statistics into a salable article.

Professional writers follow the rule we've just observed— dramatizing one fact or experience to win readers with a catchy title and lead. For example, you as a writer decided that a certain professional man must have had experiences dramatic and human enough for reader interest. Law, medicine, education, religion, science—these are fields in which the personal experience interview will pan a high run of gold. You start by asking this man or woman: "What was your most amusing... pathetic ... tragic case?" or "What do people in your business (or profession) do for relaxation and diversion?" or "Are there any unsung heroes in your profession (or business)?"

A doctor begins with some pathetic cases, some amusing cases, some tragic cases. Usually the ones he considers most interesting don't provide the best article material—they're too technical. But if you have the right man or woman, you're bound to come to a tale that matches your notion of a highly dramatic case with a headline lure.

Or you can tackle personal experience subjects by investigating unusual categories and fields of work. You wonder, for instance, what a subway change-booth attendant does with her time between 2 and 6 A.M. Has she ever seen a major crime? Has her life ever been threatened, sitting as she does all alone, night after night? Since she must keep herself locked in her tiny booth, what does she do to pass the time? What does she read? Is she allowed a radio and if so does the third-rail current interfere by causing static?

Any trade, industry or profession is apt to produce a highly interesting personal experience if you'll only use your curiosity. While taking notes, keep a sharp ear open for that one big highlight you can dramatize in the lead.

When and how to use anecdotes

So far in this Lesson we've studied types of articles, sources of ideas, analyzed titles for their power to attract readers, and discussed effective leads. We haven't talked, however, about an essential feature of many good non-fiction pieces—anecdotes.

What is it that brings stories about people to life? Is it what happens to them? As far as the basic structure of the piece is concerned, the answer, naturally, is yes. But one of the strongest ways to hold the reader's attention and to carry him along is by means of the anecdote. (An anecdote is described by the dictionary as "A short, entertaining account of some happening, usually personal or biographical.")

Take that story of the sinking of the *Titanic*; leave out the anecdotes and you have a series of newspaper bulletins, nothing more. Interesting, yes; sad, yes; but gripping—no. Use of anecdotes is vital to the writing of bright, readable stories about people, as evidenced by this article by John J. Green, an FWS instructor, from the *Famous Writers Magazine*:

When Patti, my small granddaughter, came home after her third day in kindergarten, her mother asked her what the class had done. "We showed and telled," she said, her blue eyes sparkling with the thrill of this new experience.

As my daughter told me about it afterward, I realized I had the lead for an article I wanted to do about non-fiction. And I couldn't help admiring the teacher who had introduced this five-year-old and her classmates to one of the first and most important precepts of factual storytelling.

If you want to work with factual material, either in magazine articles or books, you, too, should learn the show-and-tell principle. It's fine to *tell* the reader the facts—their importance can't be overemphasized—but when you can *show* him what you're talking about with anecdotes illustrating your facts in action, you'll have done the perfect job.

Of course, the anecdote isn't new; it's been around a long time. Lincoln was one of the greatest practitioners of the art and the technique was old in his day. Remember the parables of Biblical times? And Aesop, too, did pretty well with his fables. Basically, these early stories, whether you call them parables or fables, are anecdotes.

Today, the show-and-tell technique applies to almost every type of non-fiction writing. It works better in some than in others, but always it works. Let's take a specific example.

Bruce Catton is recognized as an authority on the Civil War. Let's look at how he handled the events of April 14, 1865, in *U.S. Grant and the American Military Tradition*.

"Destiny has a way of working while people look the other way. A man will make a snap judgment on some matter of no importance whatever—he will decide, for instance, whether or not he will go to the theater with friends on a certain evening—and this decision, which seems to concern nothing more than the way a few leisure hours are to be spent, will affect all the rest of his life, and the course of a nation's history as well.

"On Good Friday in 1865—April 14 by the calendar—U.S. Grant had such a decision to make. President and Mrs. Lincoln were to go to Ford's Theater to see a popular actress in a so-so play. The President did not particularly want to go, but there was a holiday mood on the town, the theater management had announced that he would be present, and he felt that he could hardly get out of it. Would General and Mrs. Grant care to go along?

"Grant liked the theater well enough, but on this evening, less than a week after Lee's surrender, he and Mrs. Grant were anxious to get to Burlington, New Jersey, where their older children were in school. Also, when the Lincolns visited army headquarters at City Point that spring, Mrs. Lincoln had been nervous, irritable and in truth quite hard to get along with, and Mrs. Grant did not especially want any more of her company just then. So Grant made his excuses, and that

The Presidential Box at Ford's Theater, Washington, D.C., where Abraham Lincoln was assassinated.

evening he and Mrs. Grant took the train; and before he went to bed that night Grant learned that he (or, more accurately, Mrs. Grant) had made one of the most momentous decisions of his life.

"For John Wilkes Booth was also of the party at Ford's Theater that evening, and he carried out the monstrous scatterbrained plan which had taken him there. If Grant had been in the box with the President, he almost certainly would have been murdered. Booth had included him in his program for the evening. . . .

"All in all, because he went to New Jersey instead of to the theater, Grant got twenty years more life, became President of the United

States, knew the pinnacle of fame, and bewilderment and disillusion as well, left his great name to one of the shabbiest eras in American history, and missed the apotheosis that bore Lincoln aloft as in a chariot of fire once Booth's derringer had done its work."

In still another field, medical and health writing, the anecdote can be the real life of a piece. But here, it isn't just an anecdote, it's a "case history." The trick is to make it "human" at the level of the lay reader.

One of the most prolific of all non-fiction writers was the late Dr. Louis E. Bisch, a pioneer in psychiatry, who knew how to present his findings to the lay reader. In one article, "How Childlike Are You?", he showed how hangovers from childhood can make people act more like children than the adults they are. Here's one anecdote he used to illustrate his theme:

"I was out driving with a friend not long ago. The traffic was not especially heavy, but he kept getting out of line, weaving and tooting his horn as though we were headed for a fire. But we were not going any particular place—only out for recreation.

" 'You make me nervous, Fred,' I finally said. "What's the rush? We've got the whole afternoon ahead of us.'

" 'You know,' my friend replied, not in the least offended, 'my wife complains about the same thing. I sometimes give her fits. You're a psychiatrist. What's wrong with me?'

" 'If you want the truth,' I said, 'you drive like an adolescent who wants to draw attention to himself—to show off.'

" 'Is that it?' he said. And then there was a silence for a while. 'I believe you've got something there,' he finally said. 'I was like that when a kid. I was always doing outlandish things to make people notice me. I always wanted to be in the limelight—it's strange I never linked the two together.' "

Where can *you* find anecdotes to illustrate your articles? They're all around you. Perhaps a story in your local paper has an angle you can adapt. Possibly you overhear a conversation in the local supermarket that's ready-made. When you're hot on the trail of a subject, research the published material in that field. Often you'll come up with a nugget.

Suppose you're working on a piece about domestic animals. You have ample material to illustrate their lovable qualities, but you're short on anecdotes, showing the headaches they cause. So you hopefully start reading newspapers. And you find this Associated Press item from the West Coast:

"Robert Hall was on a stepladder painting his kitchen when a shaggy dog wandered in through an open door.

" 'Scram,' said Hall.

"The dog wagged his tail.

" 'Get outta here!' Hall commanded.

"The dog stepped toward the ladder.

"Hall waved a bucket of paint thinner at the dog. There was an explosion. The dog scrammed. The service porch caught fire. The kitchen caught fire. Hall scrambled down the ladder and called the fire department.

"The water-heater pilot had ignited the paint thinner, firemen said in reporting the incident. Hall said the damage will cost him $2,800."

And while this little story from life could be worked into a piece on animals, it would be just as effective if you were doing an article on offbeat insurance claims or on unusual accidents in the home.

Newspaper columnists offer a rich field for research, too. You might be able to use this anecdote from Robert Sylvester's column, "Dream Street," in the New York *Sunday News*:

"The other day a truck, a cab and a private car all managed to ram each other at Fifth Avenue and 48th Street. The three drivers were using some pretty strong language. A newcomer to the on-lookers' circle asked: 'Anybody hurt?'

" 'Not yet,' said another bystander."

Walter Wagner had a fine example of an anecdote with a real point in "He Finds Fortunes in Your Future" in *True*, the story of Herb Saxton's unusual occupation. Here's how Wagner started the piece:

"The burly, full-blooded Oklahoma Cherokee, 15 minutes after ending his shift as an oil-field roughneck, was already half-drunk as he weaved to a seat in the bus heading for Tulsa. He was mean and he was quick-tempered, and he had been followed persistently for two days by dapper Herb Saxton, who had been hoping to catch him privately in a sober moment.

"Saxton, an ex-lawyer turned professional hunter of missing heirs, who has handled $20 million in unclaimed estates—to the financial gain of the recipients and the eminent satisfaction of himself—slipped into the seat next to the juiced oil worker. 'You're a missing heir entitled to an estate worth $60,000,' Saxton told him.

"The news had the impact of an arrow shot into the sea. The Cherokee looked at Saxton through glazed, uncomprehending eyes. He pulled out a pint and, after another swallow, offered the bottle to Saxton. 'Have a drink,' he commanded.

"Saxton politely refused.

" 'I said, have a drink,' the man repeated more insistently.

"When Saxton again turned him down, the roughneck slipped a .45 from his jacket and held it parallel with the pint. 'You bastard,' he bellowed. 'You won't drink with me because I'm an Indian!' "

This Wagner story gets off to a fast start through the author's use of people. He shows you the picture as he sets the scene and introduces his main character. And note how simple bits of dialogue give added punch to the story.

I've covered several ways to use anecdotes in articles and some of the places where such material can be found. But there's another source I haven't mentioned, though I used an example at the beginning of this piece.

To be honest, I *created* my opening anecdote. I do have a granddaughter named Patti, she has blue eyes and did go to kindergarten. Those are facts. But Patti didn't say, "We showed and telled," and I'll probably have some explaining to do when she reads this article and objects to being quoted ungrammatically. But the anecdote *did* make the point I wanted and it *did* give me a lead for this piece. And there's no reason why you shouldn't go and do likewise.

In reading this article by John Green, you will note that the anecdotes he uses are not only varied in theme and content but are also chosen carefully to prove various points. It goes without saying the writer always selects the proper anecdote to fit the proper place in his article. For instance, a good writer would never attempt to emphasize a serious point by including a lighthearted anecdote nor would he become heavy or serious when he wanted to inject a note of humor.

Good taste and common sense indicate the kind of anecdote the writer needs to embellish his piece. And always, the more anecdotes he has in his research files or at his fingertips, the better equipped he is to write an article rich in human interest.

Stockpile your information

According to the type of story, I get a great deal of material by mail. If, say, it's an industry story, companies are always willing to send material. If you're working a bit in advance (as you should on every story), you can have it all in by the time you're ready to start writing.

I rely more on mail than telephone because I know, usually several months in advance, what articles are going to be done at which time. Right now (this is October) I'm working on a story to be written in March. I'm getting the material all lined up so when March comes along, there'll be pile of information ready for the kick-off. I have another piece in the works now that I won't do for another two years. Nevertheless, I've started collecting material for it.—J.D. Ratcliff

Putting copy in the "deepfreeze"

Constant revision is one of the keys to successful writing, whether the revising is done by the author or the editor. For the writer, one simple device will make revising easier and more effective. After you've finished the first draft of a piece, put it away in your desk drawer for a few days, even longer. You'll be amazed at what comes to light when you read it again.

Phrases and sentences that seemed quite adequate when you wrote them will now stand in need of repair. Paragraphs, pages, perhaps the entire piece will reveal flaws. There's nothing like putting copy in the "deepfreeze" for a while. Not only will the flaws crystallize but also become so obvious that you'll wonder how you missed them in the first place.—Max Shulman

Writing as-told-to stories

The steps in writing an as-told-to article are roughly these:

1. Read the newspaper clippings on the subject.
2. Spend some time with him to become familiar with his manner of speaking.
3. Discuss the story in broad, general terms and make an outline.
4. Ask questions leading to details.
5. Make a first draft.
6. See the subject again for more details.
7. Write a second draft.
8. Sit with the subject and, if possible, read the story aloud, making notes of his corrections, alterations or additions.
9. Incorporate the changes.
10. Check with the subject again.

Some subjects insist on being paid; others are satisfied only with the publicity they get and with the amateur's thrill of seeing his name in print. One will insist on sharing credit with the writer; another will prefer that only his name appears. The professional writer should not care one way or the other. He is not going to make a reputation with his as-told-to's, except among editors, and they will learn from other editors some estimate of his ability.—Richard Gehman in *How To Write and Sell Magazine Articles*

Section VII

Lesson twelve

Art-of-living
and
self-help

Art-of-living and self-help articles cover an enormous field. Pieces about improving your personality, learning French in six weeks, increasing your manual dexterity or advancing yourself in a job or career appear in almost every type of magazine from mass publications like the *Reader's Digest* to those devoted solely to philosophy. The field is not only large—it's growing.

This expanding category divides into three kinds of magazine articles:

1. Art-of-living
2. Self-help
3. How-to-do-it

Under *art-of-living* come most philosophical or uplift pieces— the general topic of the adventure of being human. *Self-help* articles put this philosophy to work and boil the general down to the specific. *How-to-do-it* is a natural extension of self-help to the field of physical dexterity and the servantless household.

An art-of-living title would be "The Sense of Common Sense" or "Live Up to Your Better Self." Such philosophizing has given untold hours of reading pleasure to the American magazine public. Seldom does it come down to specifics but satisfies the urge in every human to seek a finer life. Uplift is perhaps the oldest writing topic of them all.

But if you wrote an article on how common sense might save you if you were lost in the Pacific or how to use common sense in building a swimming pool, it wouldn't be philosophy but a practical demonstration of self-help or how-to-do-it. If you wrote "Ten-Day Crash Diet" you'd be implementing the former title "Live Up to Your Better Self" through concrete, specific self-improvement, not just talking about it. Both kinds of articles would find a reading audience.

As we said before, emphasis on personal experience is nothing new. Magazine editors draw a line, however, between "self" writing on the art-of-living and the technical article that tells a reader how to do something with his hands. They know these audiences differ. Some readers like to philosophize and think about their own world: others want to be told exactly how something is done—the step-by-step of hooking a rug, needlepoint, crocheting, weaving, ceramics, wallpapering, woodworking, lathe work or spray painting. As J.D. Ratcliff says:

> The art-of-living as translated into how-to-do-it is here to stay. In an age of expensive plumbers, carpenters and journeymen, the Department of Commerce estimates that do-it-yourself work runs into ten figures annually for materials and tools alone. Dependent for the first time since frontier days on their own resources, Mr. and Mrs. Householder have become do-it-yourself addicts—and readers. There's simply no limit to their interest in such matters.

Depending on your own bent and information, and the writing market you wish to crack, you may veer toward the philosophical kind of article or toward its opposite: the pragmatic, how-to-do-it piece. This Lesson concerns the art-of-living, self-help and how-to-do-it articles.

Art-of-living and self-help ideas

Though it is usually reflective, an art-of-living article doesn't have to be about religion or philosophy. Typical titles are the following from a single issue of the *Reader's Digest*:

"Do Your Children Run Your Home?"
"Interview With an Immortal"
"The Light in the Window"
"Far Horizon, and the Mountains Beyond"

The first title involves ways of living *with* your youngsters, not *for* them. Subheads disclose the contents: "Were they babied too long?", "Is it easier to indulge than to discipline?", "Is it easier to serve than to train children?", "Are you afraid of a showdown?", "Parents have to work as a team" and so on. Although the article should be tightly written, with plenty of specifics and pertinent anecdotes, nothing can be laid down as an unbreakable rule of a one-two-three, step-by-step procedure, as in how-to-do-it-yourself pieces. The author brings up the topic, which is art-of-living, discusses it philosophically, suggests an attitude (in this case in favor of a little discipline), and tells anecdotes which keep the fire going, but do little more.

"Interview With an Immortal" is a remembrance of Rudyard Kipling by a young American who had the pleasure of Kipling's company for a day toward the close of the famous British author's life. It's a rambling recollection rather than an interview,

A day-long chat with Rudyard Kipling provided the basis for an inspiring art-of-living article.

but it fulfills the definition of an art-of-living article because Kipling "offered more than advice—he gave something of himself to carry away." When the reader "takes something away with him," preferably uplift and almost always on the optimistic side, you're in the art-of-living field.

An article like "The Light in the Window" is even more typical of art-of-living writing. The piece begins: "I met him first on a summer day in 1936...." It is the story of a poor shoemaker with pride in his neighborhood (which was no longer tops) and his trade (which was lowly) but whose shining example gave the author the right to close the piece this way: "If you have inherited a prideful tradition, you must carry it on; if you haven't, then start building one now."

Hal Borland's "Far Horizon, and the Mountains Beyond" is a reminiscence of a Colorado boyhood. To a youngster of nine it was a land of mountains where anything was possible—a kind of forever, reaching to the very rim of the world. Later in life, long after The Place had been sold, Borland went back to the mountains to see if the magic were still there, to "measure myself against the horizon I knew in youth and to see if there still were mountains. There were." Uplift, philosophizing, goodness, optimism and hope—all these essential ingredients of the art-of-living formula are stirred with nostalgia to bring guaranteed readership.

Let's go back to examine the openings of the four art-of-living titles. We started with "Do Your Children Run Your Home?":

Family and friends had gathered to admire the first-born in a young family. One guest, the father of three teen-agers, pointed to the sleeping infant. "He looks helpless, but don't be fooled," he said. "There lies a potential tyrant. He is plotting right now to run you and this house for the next 18 years."

An anecdotal lead, and a good one, because it's provocative. The next, "Interview With an Immortal":

The year was 1935, the month was June, the English weather was blue and gold. The world was young, and so was I. But, driving down from Oxford in the old Sunbeam I had borrowed for the occasion, I felt my assurance deserting me.

It makes you want to go on reading because, in its simple, brief way, it sets up a suspenseful situation, and suspense is one of the sharpest of reader lures.

Try the lead of the third article, "The Light in the Window":

I met him first on a summer day in 1936. I had rushed into his dingy little shop to have new lifts put on my slipper heels. He greeted me cheerily, "You're new in the neighborhood, aren't you?"

Happiness, humility, optimism, the goodness of life bubble over the edges of most art-of-living pieces.

Consider the happy nostalgia of Hal Borland's "Far Horizon, and the Mountains Beyond":

Sometimes when I climb to the top of the hill behind my house in the Berkshires I look west and see, 2,000 miles and 40-odd years away, The Place—our old homestead on the high plains of Colorado. It is like the times when, as a boy, I climbed to the top of the hay-stack and looked to the horizon, far away in all directions. Over to the west were the Rocky Mountains—sometimes I could see them— not actually, but in the same way that I could see tomorrow or next summer or myself grown up.

You know this is going to warm your heart and send you back to your own childhood. The dreamy, nostalgic, reminiscent ap-proach helps fix this mood, then goes on to a marvelous descrip-tion of what a raw and primitive land, part of the great buffalo range, was like 40 years ago "... acres of treeless and waterless grassland ... 30 miles from town, six miles from a fence...."

Another type of opening to art-of-living pieces is the "you" approach. Example:

Maybe you've wondered about your chances of mining a four-carat diamond right here in the United States. Well, I did just that in the diamond hills of Arkansas. I paid a daily fee which allowed me to go diamond prospecting—and I won!

This is anecdotal, but it starts with "you've" and "your." Nothing hits a reader like the word "you" and its close relatives. Adding this sure-fire "self" hook to the sure-fire anecdotal lead gives you an unbeatable opening.

Every art-of-living article *must give the reader encourage-ment*. You will get only rejection slips if you adopt the negative approach. Editors will tell you they can spot a beginner every time because his examples, anecdotes and illustrations are nega-tive. For example:

"Sally prided herself on always speaking frankly and now she hasn't a friend to her name" ... *negative approach*. "Ruth did this and that and Phillip married the other girl" ... *negative approach.* "George was next in line for promotion but he lost out because" ... *negative approach.* Don't use it for an art-of-living article that you want an editor to buy.

Another fundamental rule in writing self-help and do-it-yourself prose is: Stay away from the passive voice!

For example, don't write: "The boat should then be scraped with ..."

Write: "Then scrape your boat with ..."

Passive voice has an apologetic air. It literally backs into the task at hand. Unsure writers use passive voice to an alarming degree, and editors can quickly spot their weakness.

Which of these two phrases is more direct?

The concert is scheduled to be given by Miss King ...
Miss King will give the concert ...

The second, of course. The reader is quickly introduced to the principal subject, Miss King. This is forthright: this is fact. No beating about the bush when you start with the person's name, follow it with the principal verb, then say immediately what the subject is doing or acting upon.

We don't mean to say, of course, that passive voice should *never* be used or that there's a permanent rule against it.

Mr. Stewart was killed in an accident is the natural way to write this particular fact. You wouldn't want to write: *The automobile killed Mr. Stewart* because that gives human qualities to the auto. Nor should you write *The driver killed Mr. Stewart* because it was the combination of driver and automobile.

As with other kinds of articles, the self-help piece needs a catchy title and lead.

Here are a few titles that would attract readers:

"Don't Stop, Don't Look, Just Marry"
"How to Live 365 Days a Year"
"Stop Breaking Your Heart!"
"Try Giving Yourself Away"
"Can You Read What You Write?"
"They Count Their Wealth in Sons"
"Making Habits Work for You"

Some of these suggest art-of-living philosophy without much practical instruction. Others come close to the opposite extreme, the step-by-step "how-to" piece. But all the titles are provocative, as are their leads. They trap the reader, and persuade him to read on.

An art-of-living article

As an actual example of this type of article, here is a prize-winning piece from *McCall's*, "The Survival of a Family," written by Mary Baumeister while she was a student in the Famous Writers School. Apart from its effectiveness as a story, it is beautifully constructed: the parts go together like the components of a fine watch.

While a student in the Famous Writers School, Mary Baumeister wrote an effective art-of-living article about her family's triumph over adversity which was bought and published by *McCall's*.

Notice the spare yet readable style. There are few modifiers, and while the words are simple, each means exactly what it should mean. The whole article flows so easily we don't realize what care has gone into the preparation.

We suggest you read it twice, the first time straight through, to enjoy it as a fine piece of work; the second time analytically, pausing to read our marginal comments.

The first two words, "Growing up . . ." make an effective hook. Everybody is interested in the process of growing up. The readership of *McCall's* (mostly women with children) is particularly so. This is a good example of slanting a lead toward a special readership.

Growing up, for most people, is a gradual experience, the culmination of a long series of happenings and circumstances. In my family this was not the case. My brother and I were suddenly called upon to act as adults while we were still children. My mother was asked to become more of a woman, to undertake hardships beyond most human endurance. All three of us can name the day that maturity was thrust on us.

Two paragraphs are given over to a description of a family, especially the father. Yet we are told nothing of what the story is about. The crux of the piece is deliberately delayed.

We were a normal if slightly zany family. I always considered that we had much more fun than my friends and their families, because we did things spontaneously. Trips, picnics, projects, buying a pet or a boat or renting a house seemed to be done on the spur of the moment. My father, an Air Force colonel, was one of the warmest, most unselfish human beings on earth, and yet beyond any doubt he was also the backbone of our family. Loving us and loving life, he was still a man whose word was law, and we all knew it. He had that rare quality of being truly interested in people and therefore had a deep understanding of friends and family and all their problems. Most people listen just in wait to say something of their own. He listened to hear. Our house seemed always to be filled; our friends and my parents' friends dropped in constantly and knew they were welcome. My folks were people who enjoyed people, and they were passing this on to us. It was a tradition we enjoy to this day.

"Tragedy struck . . ." Another clue. We're still being teased; we want to know *what* tragedy—and eagerly read on. But the answer is still held back.

At the time tragedy struck our family, we were stationed in Madison, Wisconsin. My father always worked tremendously hard. He was a respected officer, and men sought his opinions. He had helped develop the use of electronic equipment for the Air Force when he was stationed at the Pentagon. In Madison, he was under great pressure in his job and was working long hours every day. In addition, he was taking engineering courses at the University of Wisconsin, to improve his understanding of a project in which he was involved. He had also just received orders to go to Korea and was under the added strain of settling us in a home and in surroundings where we could manage easily without him for at least a year. Whatever spare time he had left over he spent doing things with us when he should have been resting.

"And then, suddenly. . ." Yet another teaser.

And then, suddenly, it was all more than his body could stand. He came home from the office one day with a blinding headache and that night was rushed to the hospital, almost unconscious. He had suffered a severe cerebral hemorrhage. It was several hours before the doctors would even let my mother see him. They did so then only because they were convinced that he was dying, his heartbeat was so faint. In his room she went down on her knees, and with all the faith she had, she prayed throughout the entire night. In the morning, the doctors were amazed to find my father still living.

He was transferred to Walter Reed Hospital, where my mother was asked to decide his fate. An operation could be performed, which might save his life. Without it, there was no question that he would die. But undergoing it would mean that he would suffer paralysis of his left side, the loss of his memory, and he would be a completely altered personality. It was a terrible decision to have to make for someone else. My mother wanted him to live more than anything in the world. She adored him. But to change his life completely, to make him a different person was a wrenching, heartbreaking thing to do. Here was a man who had been physically and mentally active every day of his life. The few times he had been ill, with a severe cold or some such infirmity, he had been dismal. He had to be doing constantly. My mother feared what being bedridden for years might do to him. But she took the chance. She wanted him to live.

The operation took fifteen hours and was technically successful. It saved my father's life, but the trials had just begun. The frightening life-and-death part of the drama was over; now the real work began.

My mother had been a well-cared-for—what you might even call a pampered—woman. She had someone to do the housework and heavy ironing and rarely did her own grocery shopping. Life had radically changed with my father's illness. She was now the acting head of the family; all decisions were up to her—finding a new home, running a household, being a father and mother to my brother and me. But most of all, she was the one who had to give my father faith when he awoke from the anesthetic and discovered his paralysis, a mind that couldn't remember, a lost will to live. After recovering from her initial shock, she responded as I think few women with her background could have done.

She began by finding us a home. A housekeeper was hired for the sole purpose of being at home when my brother and I returned from school. He was then twelve, and I was seven. Mom was at the hospital from early in the morning until just before dinner time. She returned in the evening, cooked our dinner and took us back to the hospital with her. In her little spare time, she handled the cleaning, laundry and shopping. She was lucky to get four hours' sleep a night.

As I look back over those difficult years, I think that the finest and most courageous contribution my mother made was in making us understand. She explained what it was to have to be adult when you were a child, the importance of accepting things as a grown-up, and how to make the very best out of each situation. She knew one parent

"Severe cerebral hemorrhage . . ." Now we know what happened. We've been introduced to the family and we want to find out how they dealt with this tragedy. If the story had started with the crux, "My father had a cerebral hemorrhage. . ." we wouldn't care nearly as much.

"An operation . . ." the classic dilemma. No matter which decision Mother makes, the result will likely be tragic.

". . . but the trials had just begun." For the first time we see the form the rest of the story is to take: a double fight—the fight for Father's life and the fight to save the family's life.

". . . the acting head of the family." Mother has never had to face any great strain; will she be equal to this one?

". . . four hours a night." In this sentence and elsewhere the writer shows us the weight that Mother had to support.

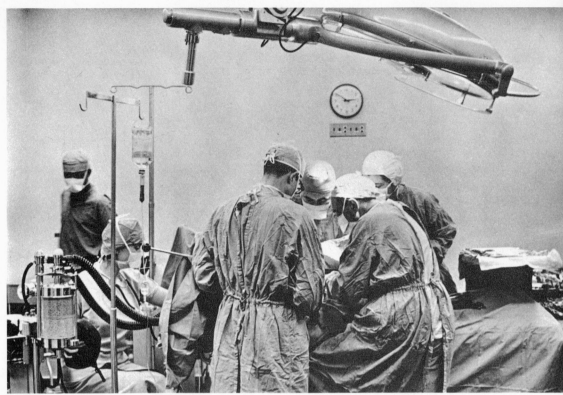

"The operation took fifteen hours and was technically successful.
It saved my father's life, but the trials had just begun. The frightening
life-and-death part of the drama was over; now the real work began."

"She convinced us things
would get better." In
addition to carrying her
own load, she helped the
children with theirs.

"My brother was
chosen . . ." This is a nice
use of specific facts to
explain the depth of
meaning behind "Being
adult . . ."

was not enough in a close family used to two. But she told us that she
was to be mother and father for a while, that her decisions were the
ones we would abide by and her word was law. She also taught us
that just because someone you love becomes very ill and changes,
you do not stop loving him or remembering the person he was. She
convinced us that things would get better, that there was never a
chance they wouldn't.

Being adult, we found, meant doing many things you did not want
to do and not being able to do things you wanted to. My brother was
chosen for the crew in his high school and was delighted. But after
several workouts, he discovered that the practices would be too time-
consuming. He had taken on a man's job at home, trying to take
some of the pressures from my mother's shoulders. He did much of
the driving to and from the hospital; he did yard work, started dinner
with my doubtful help, and in general gave as much assistance as a
teen-age boy could. He said nothing about dropping crew, although
it must have been a great disappointment to him.

For quite a few months, my father showed little response to our visits. We were stricken by the change in him. His interest in everything seemed totally gone. To compound difficulties, we learned that he would probably never walk again. He could; in fact, barely hold his head up or sit without assistance. Every movement was a personal agony, not only physically but mentally. He had been superbly fit, and now he could not perform the smallest service for himself. The people he loved were watching him day by day in a struggle just to survive.

But survive he did! It's hard to say when the change in him actually began. But one day we suddenly realized that he had made up his mind to overcome his paralysis. After that, nothing could stop him. I remember a doctor in his room talking to him. The doctor expressed his regret that Dad would not be walking again, but said perhaps he could learn to stand unassisted with a few years of therapy. "You go to hell," Dad said, in his customary Irish boom. "I'll outrun you in a few years."

It has been sixteen years since the operation. Not only does my father sit up and hold his head up; he walks well by himself. He drives a car, can cook a meal, works with his electronic equipment and has been asked frequently by members of the Air Force to return in an advisory capacity to the Pentagon. He was retired as a full colonel from a lieutenant colonel when the doctors long ago decided that his body and mind would never function normally again. He is now enjoying his retirement; he has time to do things he never did before. My parents travel somewhere exciting each year—Aruba, Saint Thomas, Florida—and now have their eye on Europe. His pace was slowed down by this illness, doubtless, but his spirit was not. He overcame what were thought to be insurmountable odds, and he did it with raw courage, faith and a whole lot of fight.

He is grateful for the help he had—a wife who truly stood by him "for worse" and who has benefited by it. She grew up in her own way. She showed us and the world how tough even the loveliest and most feminine woman can be. My brother and I grew up. We grew up quickly and with adult responsibility, but it never hurt us a bit.

Thank God for families. They are the strongest units on earth if they are good ones. And one of the ways to become a good family is to be put to a test. I think ours passed with flying colors. Now that I have my own family, I hope I may bring to my husband and our two young sons the meaning of courage and endurance, of love through hardship. I think I can. I had two good teachers.

In this article, the author says practically nothing about herself. Had she done so, she would have had to say, in effect: "I was brave too." This comment would have seriously weakened a fine piece about one family's triumph over adversity.

"My father showed little response . . ." By refocusing on Father, the new family image is complete.

"Sixteen years . . ." A dramatic jump in time is used effectively by the author to emphasize the dramatic recovery of her father. The jump also sets the stage for the wrap-up of the article.

"She grew up . . ." This is an excellent playback to the theme of the opening sentence. Actually, every member of the family grew up at the same time.

"Thank God for families." A warm and inspiring close.

Next: how-to-do-it articles

In *Writer's Digest,* free lance V. Lee Oertle starts a piece this way:

You've never heard of me. None of my fiction has appeared in the top magazines. I've never had a three-parter in the *Post,* or sold a television play. Yet quite possibly you've read one of my articles in the supermarket or mechanics magazines. Never, probably, had you noticed the by-line. Why should you? It was the subject that interested you, induced you to stop and see "How to Patch a Plastered Wall" or "How to Build a Backyard Incinerator."

There's a great gap to be filled in the practical education of a skill-conscious population. And it's you, the unknown free lance, who has a good chance of filling in the blank spaces. The current trend of the city dweller to move out into single-unit suburbs has opened up a tremendous potential for do-it-yourself articles. Mr. Average Home Owner wants to know how to stop the dripping faucet, how to build that patio, and how to perform a thousand other common tasks that might confront someone fresh from a desk at the insurance company. The American Male, it seems, is not quite the jack-of-all-trades his wife expects him to be. He'll study *Household* on the sly (or one of the other top service mags) then make a big show of building a little brick something.

This is the field for writers interested in making extra money especially if you are still working toward your first sale. Editors will buy from the unknown as readily as from the name pro, and the word rates compare favorably with the top slicks. The market is big and varied including women's and men's service magazines and general family. Ideas range from small improvement jobs around the house covered in 50—100 words to major articles on such subjects as building a house, a pool—complete remodeling jobs, etc.

It would be stretching it to call myself a professional writer, despite my seventy-odd sales to the how-to market in the past seventeen months. I make my living in the plastering business, and if there is anything further from the literary world I never heard of it.

Like the reader of Westerns, the reader of how-to-do-it pieces comes to expect formula phrases and plots. This is the method most how-to-do-it writers have adopted:

First paragraph: The subject must be named immediately. Then the reader is told why he should want to tackle it. Then follows a list of reasons why the reader should do it the writer's way.

Second paragraph: List of materials, tools and time required. You may want to give estimated cost (but double-check it before press deadline!). You may even suggest where to buy things.

Third paragraph: The job itself—you start with the first step and go right through, pausing at significant operations to explain precisely how, what and when. This is pure expository writing and therefore will probably be done in the present tense.

Almost all how-to-do-its require artwork of some sort, a photograph (showing the author of course) or simply a rough sketch which the editor will then have redrawn by a staff artist.

Most how-to articles have some of these things in common:

1. New products, how they can be used, where and when.
2. Short cuts or savings in business, or home procedures.
3. New or better methods of performing common tasks.
4. Basic instruction in the arts and crafts, gardening or sewing, homemaking, shop, maintenance or outdoor living.

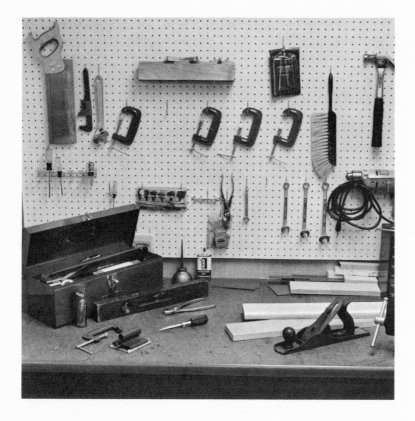

Many how-to-do-it articles have their beginnings in the author's home workshop.

When you write about familiar subjects, there's less risk of error than if you discuss a new product. On the other hand you'll sell the piece faster if there's a new angle, something frankly unusual about the subject. Gadgets, hobbies, improvements—your own house, your neighbor's, are bubbling with do-it-yourself sales potential for the article writer. All you have to do is be observant.

Thumbing through a handyman magazine, you come upon a story about refinishing table surfaces that's so badly conceived it makes you mad. You've done more than your share of wood-work and you *know* what you're reading is nonsense. So you get out your camera, begin with information about a new kind of electric sander you saw yesterday in a catalogue, write the piece the way it should be written and send it to *Popular Mechanics*. Seven days later you have not only stormed the no-sale barrier but are $175 richer!

Now, how do you go about writing how-to-do-it pieces? The lead is vital, as in all articles. So is the title. Most titles of this sort begin with "How to . . ." but there are catchier ones which read something like this:

"Save Your Boat with Cover-Kote"
"You Don't *Have* to Have a Wet Cellar"
"New Uses for Scotch Tape"
"Use That Old Crankcase Oil"
"Don't Let the Birds Eat Your Berries"

The lead must be straightaway, direct, forthright. Unimpeachable honesty must strike your reader between the eyes, or you've lost him. One good way to begin is:

Whirling aluminum foil in the sun may save your berry crop this summer. It doesn't cost much, and you can set it up yourself. The only tools you'll need are a pair of scissors, some twine, a couple of high sticks and a few minutes of your time. That's little enough to pay to keep the birds from dive-bombing your blueberries and ruining your crop.

Here's another formula lead:

A new product called Cover-Kote has made its appearance in hardware stores and has more uses than even its makers claim. Many places on the metalwork of your boat develop salt-water rust and corrosion which simply won't come off by ordinary methods. Cover-Kote seems to do the trick—if you follow this easy formula.

You don't have to know every step yourself. Friends, neighbors, experts in the field will help check your procedures and probably improve them. Nor is the do-it-yourself field limited to men. Suggestions for work-easers, decorating ideas, new product uses abound in women's magazines and many general publications. One women's magazine recently carried an effective five-page article with color pictures on how to change an attic to a lovely guest room without the aid of paperhanger, plasterer, painter or carpenter other than the Man of the Family.

A backyard barbecue pit may be uninspiring to you, but if you can write a catchy how-to article about barbecues with a new slant, you may find yourself a few dollars richer and your foot in the door of a writer's market. Have you ever discovered—and applied—any new wrinkles in tool sharpening, running your office, furnishing your home, maintaining your garden, playing games, mixing drinks, tuning your piano, repairing your car or hooking a rug? Do you know a sure-fire way to save for a rainy day? Write it. Did you learn to play a musical instrument all by yourself? Tell others how.

To turn out a successful article on practical guidance, you must keep in mind two requirements:

First, your directions must be crystal clear.
Second, your directions must work for anyone, anywhere.

If the reader doesn't understand your step-by-step procedure, he won't be able to perform the operation. If your directions aren't plain to the most uninformed reader, you've done a poor job. Constantly say to yourself as you write: "If I knew nothing whatsoever about this business, would I be able to follow my own directions?" More often than not, on rereading your copy, the answer is "No." Then you should rewrite, eliminating ambiguities and simplifying language that's simple to you but Sanskrit to some.

In *Magazine Article Writing,* Ernest Brennecke, Jr., and Donald Lemen Clark say:

Before the writer begins to draft his practical article, he should go through the magazines to see where his material will meet with the most appreciative readers, and in order to get hints as to the proper length and treatment to adopt in his article. His subject will be acceptable to the general periodicals of large circulation only if it possesses "universal interest"—if it deals with things that the average American will probably want to do.

If the subject appeals only to a special group, the author will naturally have to find a magazine which reaches that group particularly, or he will find some special department in a general magazine. *Popular Mechanics,* for instance, is read by people who like to tinker with tools; women's magazines, such as the *Ladies' Home Journal, McCall's, Good Housekeeping* and *Woman's Day,* are always looking for new ideas in dressmaking, house furnishing, home entertainment, kitchen and household economy, cooking recipes and table decoration; other publications are devoted to musical practice and teaching (*The Etude* and *The Musical Observer*); others to nature lore and woodcraft, automobile repair, touring and camping, TV, radio, stamp and coin collecting, physical culture, agriculture, business, golf, tennis, aquatics and education. Every hobby has its pet journal—every profession, every trade, every occupation—and most of these journals are looking for how-to-do-it articles.

As a writer you have a never-ending source of income in the how-to-do-it article. The servantless house, the flight to the suburbs and individual dwellings, the increase in leisure time and higher standards of living have combined to give you an ever-expanding writing market.

Subjects for how-to-do-it articles range from doll-making to jujitsu. You're limited only by your own imagination, perseverance and ability as to how much you may make out of this relatively new writing bonanza.

Leaving a piece unfinished

If I have to leave a piece of writing in the middle, I try to stop in the middle of a sentence. This especially applies to telephone calls or other interruptions. By leaving a sentence unfinished, I find that I can pick up the thread of thought when I go back, for there is enough of the thought in the unfinished sentence to bring me quickly back to my subject. I learned this from a veteran writer who had used it for years. He even left a sentence unfinished when he stopped his day's work.

Like many other writers, I prefer to end the day's work in the middle of a paragraph. If I close out a paragraph or a section of a piece, wrap up a thought completely, I always have trouble getting started the next day.

Also like other writers, I start each day's work by rereading what I wrote the previous day and making penciled corrections. This brings me back to what I was doing and catches me up in the mood and flow of the story. Then I rewrite a page or two, the end of the previous day's work. This helps me to go on without a visible break in thought or continuity.

Unless the previous day's work is hopelessly bad, I never rewrite all of it at that time. It is more important to get on with the story and do major rewriting later.—Hal Borland in *How to Write and Sell Non-Fiction*

Do editors read unsolicited manuscripts?

This is a question that every beginning writer asks himself. At the back of his mind lies the thought: "If they don't read the stuff I send in, what point is there in my writing it?"

Well, look at it this way: writers need editors, but editors need writers just as much. J.D. Ratcliff has this to say on the subject of editors and writers:

"No doubt you've heard that editors are formidable people with an ingrown hatred of newcomers. Nothing could be further from the truth. Editors go to enormous lengths to develop new talent. Finding a new writer saves them money—rates for the beginner are lower. Also it gives them the thrill of discovery—and adds intense joy to the craft of editing."

However, this doesn't mean that an editor or an editor's reader will read every word of a manuscript that's obviously not up to the standard the publication requires. But you can be sure of this: your submission will get all the attention it deserves.

This is real self-help

I have two non-fiction books and a novel to my credit, plus a flock of short stories, novelettes and magazine-length "complete novels." I have found my name in the tables of contents of anthologies, heard it given radio credits and seen it flashed on motion picture and television screens. But for nearly twenty years it has been the self-help market that has bought my writing equipment, paid the cleaning woman, financed nursery school and babysitting, purchased the services of a typist and pulled me through countless financial and emotional crises.—Jean Z. Owen in *The Writer*

Lesson thirteen

Popular science and health

Avisitor from a few decades ago would be astounded at the technical vocabulary of today's average citizen and his profound curiosity about the events taking place around him. This world of surprises in which we live is the kind of world in which the popular science author thrives. Armed only with a thick notebook and an inquisitive mind (a college degree is definitely not necessary) he moves in to grind scientific jargon down to a size digestible to the layman. He is, in effect, the "pipeline" between the scientist-doctor-expert and the general public. Editors of newsstand magazines, of industrial and house organs, and of special-interest magazines are constantly looking for people who can write clearly about technical subjects.

Who are these people? Those, naturally, who like to keep up with modern life. It's the woman who reports on flavors and quantities in "A Tomato Sauce Sampler" for the restaurant-trade magazine, *Cooking for Profit*; or the author of "Computers Count the Cars," a piece on traffic problems in *Lamp*, publication of the Standard Oil Company of New Jersey.

One thing is certain; no popular technical publication will print the kind of head-spinning jargon directed to Ph.D.s; instead, they look for a combination of common sense, solid research and plain talk. And, since the practicing writer does some of his best work when he throws out what he can't use, let's see what a popular technical article is *not*—and how it should *not* be approached.

The human heart is undergoing study today with a daring that would make a 19th-century medico gasp in disbelief. Unlike research in, say, defective hearing, the heart captures the attention of young and old—and for a simple reason: if it stops, you do, too. Many devices such as plastic valves, pumps, oxygenators, have been developed—and the man-in-the-street wants to know more.

Where can he turn? Logically, the first stop would be the library. Here's a sample of what he'd find in the journal of *Surgery, Gynecology and Obstetrics:*

The oxygenator ... developed as a result of these studies ... is a large bubble oxygenator composed of five essential elements: mixing column, debubbling chamber, helix reservoir, arterial filters, and the cardiotomy aspiration chamber.

As the reader plunges on, the going gets even tougher, and it's soon apparent that the author is talking to his own trade. Overpowered by specialized jargon, our average citizen swings the other way—to the newspapers. Surely, news reportage will be factual, accurate and written in understandable language. But look at this copy from the Associated Press:

Artificial Heart Gets First Test

A team of surgeons began placing a plastic artificial heart in the chest of a patient at Texas Medical Center today. The patient was identified as Marcel DeRudder, 65, of Westville, Illinois. He has been unemployed because of his heart condition. . . . His wife, Edna, was identified as a grocery store cashier.

The technical information which follows is skimpy. The AP, aware of its obligation to stress the human-interest side of reportage, has quickly shifted its emphasis to the personal background of the patient and his family.

The reader finds a new clue

Home again, our puzzled seeker-after-knowledge chances upon an issue of *Popular Science* magazine and catches the title,

"Booster Pump Gives New Life to Failing Hearts." Quickly he turns to page 48, and learns much from the subtitle (sometimes called, in magazine parlance, the blurb):

Auxiliary heart boosters will soon be saving thousands of lives—and many more will be lengthened by amazing new pumps that replace the heart itself.

The lead or opening paragraph? A fine example of vivid, nuts-and-bolts writing:

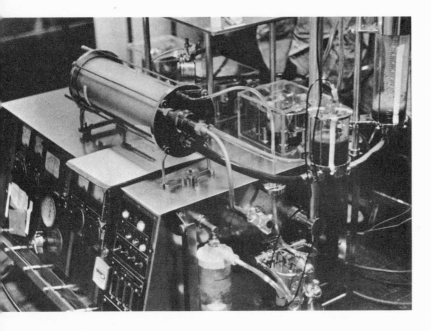

The popular science writer describing this artificial heart machine used during heart surgery, must do so in terms the average reader can understand.

On the table, a knackwurst-size plastic bulb jerked sharply in time to bursts of escaping air—once each second. Blood-colored liquid sluiced through a network of glass tubes attached to the odd apparatus.

For more than a year this weird mechanical ballet has moved through its monotonous route.... Soon an identical pump will be buried in the chest of a human patient because his heart can't pump enough blood to keep his body alive. The plastic pump—a heart booster—will take over half the natural heart's job, giving the failing organ desperately needed help.

Following hard on this dramatic opening, the popular technical article next resorts to that reliable device, dialogue.

"We have two or three patients a week who die of cardiac deficiency," says Dr. Adrian Kantrowitz, chief of surgical research at Brooklyn's Maimonides Hospital and co-developer of the heart booster, "and thousands of others die elsewhere. With the booster we can give hearts more pumping power. Many of these people won't have to die."

Pursuing the dialogue technique. even further, the author demonstrates graphically the reason why heart research is important to you.

"Sometimes a patient will get to where his heart has maybe a ten percent reserve," says Kantrowitz. "He gets dizzy when he walks up a flight of stairs. Then his reserve drops to five percent. Finally he's got no reserve. His heart can barely keep him alive. Then heart capacity drops to 99 percent of what he needs. That day he dies."

The value of a good ending

The person who'd like to write popular technical articles can learn some very valuable lessons here. The author has used a grim but effective device—he relates the ultimate catastrophe, before he talks about the progress of heart research in general. For a clincher, he ties his story into the mainstream of our lives:

But whether these advanced schemes or some yet unknown plan proves best, the artificial heart is on its way. Improvements will come over the years. Already the first tentative steps have been taken toward conquering one of man's most dreaded killers.

This is a good closing; it resounds, and maintains the same tone of urgency set at the beginning. And since openings are so important in setting the tone of an article, let's examine a few more ways to fascinate your reader from the first word. Here are some recently published examples:

Dramatic Narrative: The American Telephone & Telegraph Company, concerned over the damage being done to its underground cables by construction crews, now operates a helicopter surveillance system. AT&T's magazine, *Long Lines,* starts its article "Sentinel in the Sky" with a panoramic scene:

From 500 feet up the excavation looked like a red scar on the soft green fields. Pilot Skip Staudt banked his helicopter and descended in a series of wide circles. . . . He waved to the curious men below and nudged the copter to the ground.

Direct Quote: Eileen Burke, writing "Stain Repellents Gain Acceptance" for *Furniture Design and Manufacturing* magazine, decided on the "horse's-mouth" angle. She begins:

"Within five years any furniture manufacturer who doesn't offer stain- and dirt-resistant fabrics will be out of business," asserted Donald Sturtz, upholstery division merchandising manager, Baumritter Corp.

Flavor-of-the-Land: The author of "Great Wines Start in the Vineyard" was faced with the problem of making an agricultural weed-killer interesting. His solution—choose an area of the country where the product is in use, and appeal to the nature-loving element in all of us:

HAMMONDSPORT, N.Y.—Autumn comes early to this hill country, where original settlers described the lakes they found as the fingerprints left when the Creator's hand was extended in benediction.

Rainbow Falls is one of the scenic highlights of New York's Finger Lakes area, the state's principal wine region.

The Teaser: The *Lamp* magazine wanted to dramatize the subject of traffic control, so it ran an article beginning:

> Why would two cars be driven through the busy New York-New Jersey Holland Tunnel connected by a strand of piano wire?

There's one common element in all these leads—enthusiasm. Once you begin to investigate your topic, you'll love every minute it takes to research your facts, and you'll find yourself increasingly absorbed by the material you uncover.

Characteristics of the writer

Who is the popular technical writer anyway? He (or she) is nothing special—not an engineer or a technician. This writer combines a reasonable degree of writing skill with the ability to recognize the drama in any given development—whether it's a new kind of soap or the recent discovery that smoking causes emphysema in beagles. No matter what your interest, you should strive to cultivate the quality which Hal Borland describes in his book, *How to Write and Sell Non-Fiction:*

> That something is a combination of curiosity and what I call, for want of a better term, *constructive imagination.* He is an inquisitive fellow, but he is also a speculative person. He wants to know why something happens, how it happens, what its effects are. He also speculates about the thing that has aroused his curiosity, about its meaning, about its causes, about what would happen if other factors were added or if known factors were subtracted. He thinks all around his topic. . . . He not only dissects it; he puts the pieces together in ways other than they were originally. And he doesn't necessarily do this consciously or for a purpose; it is simply his way of thinking, his approach.

Thinking? Approach? Take one example—a widely distributed product known in various guises as hexachlorophene, pHisoHex, or G-11. It's a crackerjack remover of germs and many of us use compounds of it in our homes for sanitation, skin cleansing and personal deodorant. Hospitals use a solution of the chemical to wash down the walls of a room recently occupied by a patient with communicable disease.

Simple enough—on the surface. But the thinking technical writer moves in on this subject with a two-pronged question: Does the stuff kill germs directly, or does it starve them out by creating an area where they cannot live? Once you've developed this distinction in your mind, you're well on your way to surprising and intriguing your reader, who'll say to himself, "Golly! I never thought of it *that* way."

While medicine and health are two of the most popular science topics today, many others of equal importance are available to the writer. Electronics, mechanics and allied fields give you the opportunity to spring welcome and fascinating surprises on your readers. Your discovery of new areas can include boating, art, agriculture, photography, music, pets, foods, nature, theater—in fact, almost any subject affected by new developments.

Out of this intriguing list of subjects, what should the beginning writer choose? Here's one answer from Robert O'Brien, consultant to the *Life Science Library* and a regular contributor to *Reader's Digest, Esquire* and other national magazines:

The beginning popular technical writer *must* start writing about a subject with which he or she is familiar. Don't be tempted, early in the game, by the glamor of, say, space technology or recently developed drugs. Start with something you know about and work from there.

For instance: You're interested in 19th-century dolls; how were the ceramic heads painted and fired? Where? In what respects does the doll industry of today differ from the past?

If you follow this trail you'll soon discover that you're an expert in your field—and this is important, because the editors to whom you submit your manuscripts will gain increasing confidence in your output. What you become, actually, is a reporter—a *spotter*—who dramatizes a development that's taking place under our noses, but which you alone recognize for its importance.

Virtually all popular technical editors will agree with this point of view; but these editors often have an even greater problem. Many times the writer of a highly competent piece will submit it to the wrong publication.

"We read everything that comes to us," says Art Mikesell, editor of photography, boating and general science for *Popular Mechanics,* "and we're always looking for new writers who can become regular contributors. But too many 'over-the-transom' manuscripts betray a lack of knowledge about the subjects we cover and the readership we're trying to reach.

"Whether the writer is gunning for us or another magazine in the same field, he's *got* to read what's selling—discover for himself where the market is for his material. Otherwise, he's liable to send a perfectly good piece to the wrong publication and suffer an undeserved rejection."

Some editorial rules to follow

Once you've decided on your subject area and the type of publication you're aiming at, there are a few simple rules to follow—and your editors will love you for observing them:

Research gathered for an article on a new product, whose success necessitated additional railroad sidings at the plant, may later prove useful for a separate piece on how railroads help business.

1. *Emphasize a new slant or approach.* Like the inventor of striped toothpaste, you don't have to discover something radically new—just find a way to present your idea differently and urgently. Not too long ago a newsstand magazine ran an article on centuries' old ways of finishing furniture, and it was so popular that the readers demanded a follow-up!

2. *Research and organize carefully.* Gather all the material you can, but build that all-important outline in keeping with the special approach you've adopted. For example, an industry near your home has added a railroad siding because a new product is a tremendous success. Stick to the product—but keep the material you've gathered on the new tracks. One day you might want to do a piece under the title, "Railroad Spurs Keep Business Going." Never throw out "useless" research; it can come in handy at a later date.

3. *Create strong openings and endings.* Your opening can be one of several kinds; we've already seen an example of the "strong word picture"—the heart pump compared to the knackwurst, the bursts of escaping air. But "visual" openings don't always make your point effectively. Sometimes the "gee-whiz" fact does it better.

Popular Science writer Bill Taylor kicks off a piece on the dilemma of the new-car buyer with this attention-getting statement: "The man who wouldn't think of buying a $60 suit without trying it on often shells out 50 times as much for a car he's never driven."

Your ending must be equally resounding; it must tie up the loose ends. If your reader doesn't hear the door slam behind him, he'll soon forget that he's been to your house. Here's how Jacques-Ives Cousteau concludes a *National Geographic* article on life—human, sustained life—under the sea:

We are now planning Conshelf Four.... We are confident that within a few years, we will entirely eliminate ties to the world above. Then, for the first time, oceanauts will have true freedom of the deep.

Department of Agriculture is a source

Where can a beginning article writer dredge for popular science ideas? Many a fine magazine article on nutrition and health has come from a U.S. Department of Agriculture source on the growing, harvesting or processing of food and its by-products. Industry likewise issues pamphlets on all manner of scientific, engineering and medical advances. J.D. Ratcliff expands this thought:

The scientific journals are written by professional men and women in the field for their colleagues' eyes alone. Much of what they write is gibberish to the average reader, since the use of Latin and scientific mathematics obscures the writing. But it can usually be translated into readable English. That's where the magazine article expert comes in. He knows (or can find out) what the esoteric terms mean and put them into readable English, the stuff of which good science and health articles are made. He may even beat the scientific journals to the punch by personally covering the meeting or convention where the paper is first read.

Once the information appears in professional or scientific journals, the trade press picks it up. Let's suppose, for example, that a doctor has discovered a startling new use for a miracle drug. He tells a group of fellow physicians about it in a paper before an annual medical conference. The *American Journal of Pharmacy* covers the conference and reports the find to the pharmacists of America. You, a free-lance writer, pick up a copy of the journal and smell a feature story. It didn't come from the original medical source but from a publication for druggists who will now sell this relatively old drug for a new purpose. That's *news,* and therefore would likely make a salable magazine article for mass readership.

Sometimes a good feature will filter through a scientific or trade publication and first see the light of popular publication in a newspaper. That's why all competent magazine writers *must read a daily newspaper.* What man is there who can say how many thousands of excellent magazine pieces originated in feature stories in *The New York Times?* The number must be staggering indeed.

Extending this line of thought logically, you come to another source for popular science and health articles: current books. If a writer has discovered something unique, he may not wish to give it away in one magazine article. Instead, he may prefer to get as much mileage as he can out of it by writing an entire book. You don't have to buy his book. That's what libraries are for. But you do have to examine books, constantly. No one is going to whisper in your ear that there's a good magazine piece here. You find those things out for yourself.

In *Article Writing and Marketing,* George L. Bird inclines toward the expert as the best source for a writer:

Experts are a fine source of articles. The county agricultural agent, for example, could provide all the material needed for a piece on gardening.

The man who has achieved eminence in his field is usually a man who knows something the public would profit from hearing. Take a medical specialist. The eye specialist can tell the public how to protect its precious eyesight. The child specialist can tell parents how to protect their children from diseases of childhood. Or the specialist may be an expert automobile mechanic who can give advice on proper operation and maintenance. He may be the county agricultural agent giving advice on city gardening or rural planting. One would have to exhaust the list of trades and professions to mention all possibilities.

These experts can be approached in several ways. In each case an interview, or several, will be necessary. The free-lance writer may have an order from a magazine or newspaper, or he may only hope to sell the proposed article. Through a series of questions, enough material is drawn from the expert to support the theme of the article. The subsequent article may be signed by the free lance alone, by the two jointly, or by the expert alone.

A somewhat different idea is that of asking certain types of experts for tips on possible articles. The free lance will find that librarians, historians, curators and others can often point out feature subjects, i.e., individuals, landmarks or institutions worthy of a write-up. Among other sources where feature material accumulates are hotels, trade associations, institutions of learning; public bodies, such as boards of health, offices of city and country legislators, and water-works; and factories and distributive agencies.

What remains for the free-lance writer as a source of popular science and health ideas? A neglected but highly fruitful source for new writers is *their own experience*. Every reader has come across an article by a writer whose passionate interest has lifted the piece out of a pedestrian rut. The secret of the appeal is the writer's great inner urge to get into print on the subject. Almost always it's something he or she knows intimately from personal experience. No better idea field exists for the beginning writer.

For instance, you happen to have a bad case of hay fever. You've read articles on new antihistamines but the pieces don't, in your opinion, sufficiently dramatize the wonders of alleviating violent sneezing, coughing and choking soon after you've swallowed one tiny pill. The average person, you feel, hasn't the foggiest idea what these new antihistamines can mean to the poor victim of hay fever. You want desperately to tell the true story. You may even write it in the first person—no harm in that, since it adds the welcome pinch of "self." Within your own circumstance and experience may lie a most prolific source of popular science and health material.

Rules for science writing

Bergen Evans gives the following warnings about writing popular science:

There are two fundamental pitfalls into which most beginning free lances stumble:
1. They exaggerate.
2. They pretend great knowledge.
The facts of science are so startling in themselves that they don't need to be exaggerated. Anyone going beyond the facts isn't likely to build magazine article sales. It's far better to be on the conservative side than to be too optimistic or dogmatic. When in doubt, understate it.
By pretending to know more than you know—by using unpro-

nounceable terms, Latin names and scientific patter as though you ran it through your vocabulary every day—you commit the worst of non-fiction sins. You patronize your reader, confuse, baffle and eventually lose him.

Don't pretend to be an expert when you write popular science. Better by far to admit you're still mortal, and a lay mortal at that. Let the facts speak for themselves. You should simply be the word instrument through which the world is revealed to your readers.

An excellent set of instructions for handling the popular science article was compiled by Edwin E. Slosson while director of *Science Service* in Washington, D.C. His rules follow in part:

Don't overestimate the reader's knowledge and don't underestimate the reader's intelligence. He may not know as much as you about this particular thing—let's hope not, anyway—but otherwise he may be as bright as you are—let's hope so, anyway.

Don't try to tell all you know in 500 words. Leave some over for another time. The clean plate rule does not apply here.

Don't think that because a thing is old to you it is known to the public. Many of your readers are still living in the nineteenth century; some of them in the eighteenth. Anything new to your readers is "news" to them if hung on a timely peg.

Don't imagine that the readers of a paper are, like pupils, obliged to pretend to pay attention to you no matter how dull you may be. "First catch your reader" is the rule of successful writing.

Don't leave out the human interest. Your reader is a human being even if you are only a scientist.

Don't forget that your reader is interrupting you every ten lines to ask, "Why? What for?" or "Well, what of it" and if you don't answer his tacit questions he will soon stop reading.

Don't think that you can make your topic more attractive by tricking it out with fairy lore or baby talk or irrelevant jokes or extravagant language. Bring out its real and intrinsic interest as forcibly as you can. Set off the red fire if you like, but be sure it lights up the object instead of drawing attention away from it.

Don't say "this discovery is interesting" unless you can prove it is, and if you can prove it, you don't have to say it.

Don't suppose you must give bibliographical references to all the literature of the subject, but don't fail to give a clue by which the interested reader can get on its trail.

Don't fail to put your best foot forward or you may not have a chance to use the other foot. Note the construction of the news story in any first-class paper. It is built upon the same logical system as the symphony or opera overture. The opening paragraph gives the main point of interest, the gist of the story, just as the first movement of a musical composition expresses the theme or motif.

Don't expect the editor to explain why he objects to your manuscript. He is probably right in his verdict, but if you would make him give a reason for it he will have to invent one and it would probably be wrong.

Don't back up too far to get a running start. Remember the man who wanted to jump over a hill. He ran a mile to work up momentum and was so tired when he got to the bottom of the hill that he had to sit down and rest. So will your readers. Ninety percent of the manuscripts I've handled in twenty years as an editor would have been improved by cutting off the first page or paragraph. Yet, authors, like hens, kick on decapitation.

Don't imagine that you must add a pretty but superfluous paragraph at the end, like the coda of a sonata. The most effective close is to quit when you get through.

Don't shoot in the air. Aim at somebody. You may miss him, but you are more likely to hit somebody else than if you aim at nobody. Look out of your window and note the first person coming along the street. Imagine yourself stopping this man or woman on the sidewalk, and, like the Ancient Mariner, holding his or her attention until you have told your tale to the end.

Don't forget when you are writing for the papers that you are broadcasting to a million potential readers. But how many of them are listening in depends on how you write.

Don't refer to notes or books while writing. Read up on the subject as thoroughly as you can, and take as many notes as you need; then put away all your notes and books out of reach and next day or at least an hour later lay clean sheets of paper on a clear desk and write out what you know about it, in your own way. Afterwards, preferably the next day, read over your manuscript critically, verify your facts, correct your data, revise your English and add any essential points, but don't expect the reader to be interested in what is so uninteresting to you that you cannot keep it in mind a single hour.

Don't define a hard word by a harder word. Vladivostok is a hard word. But when a press correspondent arrives at Vladivostok he goes right on inland without stopping to explain that "This is a city south of Khabarovsk and east of Tsitsihar." So, if you want to say "calorie," say it, but don't make it worse by "explaining" it as "the quantity of heat necessary to effect a rise of temperature of one degree Centigrade of a cube of water each dimension of which is one-hundredth part of the length of a bar of platinum and iridium alloy lying in the observatory of St. Cloud." If you think you must define the calorie, say something like this, "that 100 calories of energy can be derived from three cubes of sugar or from a small pat of butter," or explain that a man needs to expend about 100 calories an hour to keep his body running, and 160 calories if he's working hard. . . .

Before you tackle a popular science article, ask yourself one

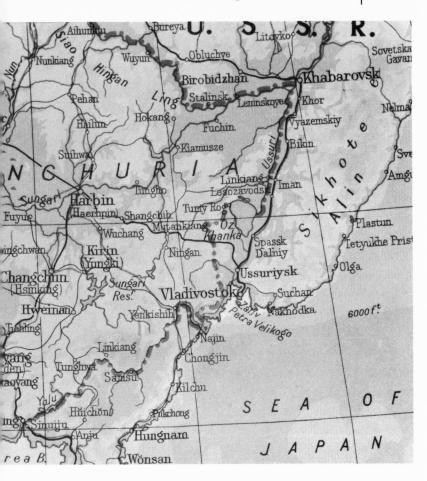

Keep explanations simple. You accomplish little by saying that Vladivostok is a city south of Khabarovsk and east of Tsitsihar.

final, penetrating question: Do I know enough in the general area of this subject to translate technical fact and statement into common English? If not, have I the perseverance to learn?

Be completely honest in your answer. If you're not wholly honest, you're already in trouble. But if you know the problem ahead and accept the tedious hours of research and self-education required, you have an excellent chance of breaking into one of the great writing realms where editors pay top prices.

Health is a powerful topic

Since all readers instinctively think of self when they read, the article on personal or public health has no peer in non-fiction. Editors like to buy a fresh, well-written piece on the common cold, whooping cough, a safe driver's eyes, safe motherhood for heart patients, how to grow old gracefully, or nutritional quackery because they know they'll get readership. Where the popular science article generalizes about the world in which the reader lives, the health article talks about the reader's own life or the life of someone near and dear.

Health is a natural for the article writer, beginner or pro. Let's look at a few issues of *Today's Health,* a magazine published by the American Medical Association for family readership. *Today's Health* is popular health, pure and simple, the simpler the better. Typical titles:

"Comeback Battle Against Stroke"
"Falls: A Big Threat to Oldsters"
"What America Needs: A Decent Breakfast"
"New Hope: Spare Parts for the Body"
"How to Avoid Sunburn"
"Six Ways to Strengthen Your Marriage"

You know right off what you're going to find under these six titles. The first two articles on strokes and falls will be avidly read by older people or families with older people around. The third is universal, but housewives in particular will want to know what medical science considers "a decent breakfast."

The fourth title about spare parts for the body is bound to intrigue the gamut of readership, since almost every family has a member with a malfunction or threat of one. Sunburn couldn't have a wider audience in view of the growing trend toward holidays and travel. Marriage problem articles invariably come near the top of any reading census.

However, not all popular health titles or leads tell the story right off. Often they tease a reader into going on, for curiosity is a powerful magnet. Wouldn't these titles from the same publication make you wonder what they were about and entice you to open the magazine to those pages?

"Let 'em Eat Hay"
"Two for One"
"Little One Late"
"How Old Do You Think You Are?"
"A New Dimension of Love"
"The Operation No One Talks About"
"Count to 100"

The first title involves food quacks who are doing a $500 million a year business with supplements, tonics and utensils they claim will cure everything from gallstones to cancer. This is an incredible story of modern quackery, deriving its title from the generous assortment of phony foods which contain alfalfa, parsley and watercress. Most of them won't do you any harm but they won't cure anything, either. The tricky title hooks you and the lead doesn't disappoint, which is important.

A piece called "Two for One" is about twins. Do twins have lower I.Q.'s? Are they always premature? Is it bad to separate them? Are twin births hazardous? Are twins of the same sex always identical? These and other answers dispel much misinformation and give the reader a fascinating fifteen minutes. The title suits and beguiles, but doesn't give the story away.

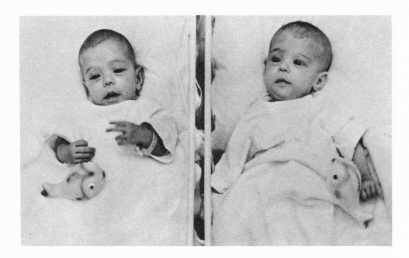

"Two for One"—this catchy title for a piece about twins is calculated to entice readers, as every good title should do.

Having a baby late in life is a blessed event that middle-aged women often talk about but seldom experience. Now, at 40, a woman is blushing to admit it's her turn to have a "Little One Late." You can wager the piece will get a thorough reading by women, though many a middle-aged husband has also wondered what it would be like to start a family in his 40's. This title is obscure but honest—and catchy.

The next title involves the fundamental process of growing old. Most people are younger than they think. By considering themselves older than they are, they actually may be hastening their own decline. While this title isn't as obscure as the others, you don't really know what the article's about until you read it.

The fifth article is most unusual—about a husband and wife whose child "wasn't just right" and what they went through when they were told, after exhaustive tests, that it never would be. The article is illustrated with unposed photographs taken during the tests, even at the moment of truth when the heart-breaking, shattering knowledge is imparted that their daughter isn't normal. The title, when you've finished the sympathetic, understanding piece, is perfect, for this couple discover "A New Dimension of Love" understood by few parents.

You wonder what "The Operation No One Talks About" can be. You think over all the embarrassing operations in the catalogue and probably turn to the article to see if you were right. Chances are you were wrong. The "operation no one talks about" is legal autopsy, frequently refused by a grieving family but essential for reconstruction and diagnosis of illnesses which cause mysterious deaths. The lead tells about a man in his mid-70's who died suddenly and whose family wisely permitted an autopsy, which revealed advanced tuberculosis. Because the disease is communicable, the discovery was most significant to members of the victim's family. Immediate tests revealed that two grandchildren already had active pulmonary tuberculosis. The title and the article complement each other perfectly.

The seventh title, "Count to 100," concerns a crusading naval surgeon whose passion for purity in drugs nearly cost him his life. It's one of the endless yet fascinating bits in the history of anesthetics, which made their debut a century ago in a crude laboratory in Brooklyn. The title refers to words of yesteryear, when doctors, as they dropped anesthetic on the patient's gauze mask, said: "Now count slowly to 100."

The first set of six titles hooked the reader by appealing to his or her interest in personal health. There was no deception: you knew precisely what you were going to read when you saw: "Falls: A Big Threat to Oldsters" or "How to Avoid Sunburn." But the second set of seven titles used a more subtle approach, for curiosity is powerful, particularly when personal health is involved. The title "The Operation No One Talks About" is a classic example of readership lure.

By no coincidence, practically all the articles whose titles we've just reviewed opened with anecdotal leads. The writer told a little story, introduced the main theme through personal experience easily identifiable with the reader, then stated the thesis:

That Americans need a decent breakfast but aren't eating it.
That medicine is making progress in replacing damaged parts of the human body.
That many food fads and phony drugs are the results of modern quackery.
That a woman in her 40's will welcome a late baby.
That autopsy should be allowed whenever a doctor asks.

The few articles that didn't start with an illustrative story stated their principles first, then quickly supported and dramatized them with case histories every reader would recognize as true and lifelike. In other words, our primary non-fiction techniques apply once again, though the category has changed from personal experience and art-of-living to popular science and health. It's amazing how the basic non-fiction writing pattern fits almost any topic.

Danger signals for article writers

Before spending appreciable work on an article—personal experience, art-of-living, popular science, health or whatever—most professionals look for seven danger signals. Instinctively they check these before they invest their time, which to them is the same as money.

1. *Is this a good subject?* Many a writer gets an idea for an article, puts together some material and a few anecdotes, then stands back and looks at his preliminary sketch. Too many times the professional then finds no single line of logic, no distinct pattern, no strong central thread, no fresh conclusion to be drawn. What has happened, more often than not, is that the writer's camera simply wouldn't focus. The topic was too large, too diffused. There were too many variables which strayed from the main theme, weakened the article's continuity, destroyed its unity.

2. *Good subject but no market?* Every once in a while a

writer will come across one of those fabulous characters who teem with color, whose anecdotes are prolific and quotable. In other words, a natural. The same applies to topics. Occasionally you strike something so fresh, so new and exciting you can't wait to get it onto paper. Yet the piece may not sell right away simply because too few readers have an interest in or knowledge of the topic, the locale, the personality or the wonderful subtleties that you yourself realize are there. The editor, knowing his audience, might read the article and reject it.

3. *Will you send it to the wrong market?* So many thousands of rejection slips have come from this mistake that you're positive you'll never make it! But all writers do, at one time or another. This is, however, one of the easier problems to avoid. A careful market analysis should do it. And you'll save postage, time, heartbreak and probably several retyping jobs if you aim your first shot carefully. Have a specific market in mind and know its style and readership before you begin to write.

4. *Is your article too long for its subject?* In other words, is it wordy? Does it go on and on? Does it lack selectivity? Is the structure compact, the execution tight? Could some rewrite man or editor cut it by one-third and lose nothing of its punch? Like the oft-quoted man who said he was writing a long letter because he didn't have time to write a short one, writers sometimes get so prolix they sabotage their own work.

5. *Is your article adequately researched?* In non-fiction the fact is king. There's no such thing as having done too much research, except as time and common sense dictate. Sometimes that one extra phone call or library visit will give your piece the precise authenticity, the one perfect anecdote, that will sell it.

6. *Is your approach really fresh?* Since there's precious little under the sun that's new, the writer must find a fresh approach to subjects. Let's say you've had an idea for a piece on animal hibernation but couldn't come up with an original angle. Suddenly in your research you discover that some animals hibernate in summer, too. This "hibernation" is called *estivation*. Its purpose is similar to winter sleep—an escape from the weather—in this case prolonged heat and drought. Precisely this fresh attack on an old topic was used for an article in the *Christian*

Science Monitor which *Reader's Digest* reprinted. John and Jean George called it "Nature's Summer Sleepers." Chipmunks, squirrels and frogs headed the cast of characters.

7. *Is your timing right?* Most intangible yet perhaps most vital of the seven self-searching questions is: What are the editors looking for now? If every magazine you pick up has an article on Alaska, put yours in the freezer for a while. There are streaks and cycles in publishing as there are in nature. When the first rockets went into outer space, the magazine business was deluged with pieces on interplanetary travel, jet propulsion and astronomy. Readers eventually rebelled. They wanted to know, but not to the exclusion of all other non-fiction. At the peak of the early space-travel enthusiasm, J.D. Ratcliff sold "The Growing Threat of Lung Cancer" which had been in the back of his head for some time. His instinct was unerring. He knew editors and readers would welcome a change from astronaut adventures.

Do you need photographs?

The nature of your article and the requirements of the publication you submit it to determine whether or not to embellish your piece with photographs. You must be the sole arbiter of whether your article has a visual side or whether words alone can do the job. Use this as a rule-of-thumb:

If you can't explain it by waving your hands at the typewriter, you need an illustration.

To find out the picture policy of a magazine, go to your library and examine one of the professional directories of editorial markets. You'll also find information on picture content, size, black-and-white versus color, and whether or not to include captions.

Be sure also to take advantage of the free "hand-out" pictures offered by large corporations. A letter to their public relations department, explaining your purpose and the kind of pictures you need, will produce results.

A competent amateur photographer can make his own "kitchen-table" shots. Many good books have been published on the subject, and your librarian can help you locate them.

Section VIII

Lesson fourteen

Special markets

Part I

In this Lesson and the one that follows, we're going to take you on a tour of special markets—those areas of writing which differ sufficiently enough so that they can be described in categorical terms. Some of the areas border on straight journalism, some are duplicative of each other, still others share certain basic features. But for the beginning writer, special markets are important because if he doesn't know about them, he is likely to waste time and effort attempting to invade the well-known markets which are difficult for any writer but the successful professional. In other words, the beginning writer tends to see his markets in publications familiar to him—the ones he subscribes to, reads and sees on the newsstands. However, there are thousands of periodicals he has probably never heard of.

Each special market includes first-rate magazines and newspapers; some pay surprisingly well, and you can be proud to have your work appear in them. But in these fields, as in others, the requirements vary roughly with the payment offered. High pay, stiff demands. As the pay goes down, so do the more exacting requirements.

The first area of writing we shall take up is weekly and small daily newspapers. Towns as small as 5,000 are likely to have at least a weekly newspaper. Since the major newspapers cover stories of statewide, national and international importance, what's left for these local publications? Chiefly, subjects such as:

Local sports, civic, political and social events.
Fires and accidents.
Police and court happenings.
Violence of any kind: murders, suicides—anything unusual involving people who live in the area covered by the paper.

Since small papers run on a small budget, their news staffs are small, too. Many correspondents are part-time—local people who know what's going on in their bailiwicks and can get details about an event. You can join them if you have a pad and pencil to make notes, a typewriter to write them up and a willingness to go out and get the story. Of course, you must know your district and the newsmakers in it, as well as the important people in social and business areas.

First, visit the editor of your local paper. He may consider an arrangement with you, perhaps on a trial basis—especially if you make clear that money is secondary because you're looking for experience. It's better to make a definite arrangement so you can cover what he wants covered and don't report an event already assigned to somebody else.

So much for the reporting side of local newspaper writing. Probably a better field from your viewpoint is feature writing for this market. But what kinds of features? Articles of interest to local readership of a local paper. Is a town landmark coming down to make room for a supermarket? Research it, interview people, get a picture or two, write the piece.

The people in the next county don't care that the "old Watson place" is going under the wrecker's ball, but everybody in Watsonville is interested. Be constantly on the lookout for stories like this. Somebody will cover it for the paper; it will be assigned on a first-come, first-served basis and you'll want to stake out an early claim.

Does one of the important people in your town have an unusual hobby? Query the editor of the paper by phone and maybe you'll get an assignment. If there isn't a story in the person himself or in his hobby alone, the combination may be salable.

The oldest inhabitant in your locality probably gets a paragraph or two every time his birthday rolls around. If you can connect him with an important local happening of years ago, you may be able to make a feature—especially if he has, say, a one-hundredth birthday coming up.

Maybe your town was important back in colonial times. If so, there might be a story here. Why was it important? Why isn't it important now? Your local library should be a font of regional information, just waiting for your attention.

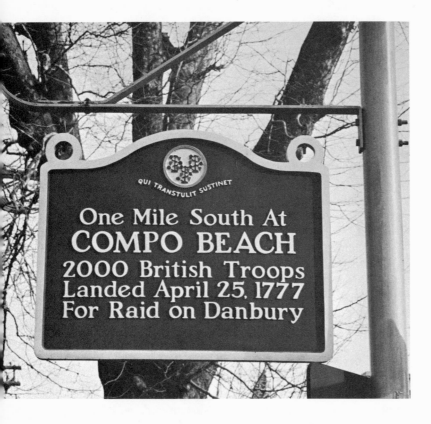

People and events related to local history are excellent subjects for newspaper features.

We've been talking about your hometown. How about the next town down the road? Those people are just as interested in local happenings, in history and in people as the citizens of your town. As long as a local newspaper is within reasonable traveling distance from your home, it's a prospect for feature articles about people and events. The pay will be small—maybe nothing at all—but you can charge your time to experience.

The Sunday supplement market

Here is another area to consider—both the regional and the national supplements. Read what Omer Henry has to say in *Writing and Selling Magazine Articles:*

Practically all major newspapers have a Sunday magazine section. It may be called the "Magazine" or the "Sunday Magazine" or it may have a title such as *Panorama, Picture, Sunday Pictorial, Empire Magazine* or *Today*. These magazines are known by the general name of Sunday supplements. Basically the supplements want stories about unusual people residing in the territory in which the paper circulates. The supplements also use articles about local points of interest.

"Local angles," says the editor of *Sunday*, a very good regional supplement issued by the *Washington Star*, "are preferred, but subjects of broad interest are acceptable so long as the interest is universal." In keeping with these criteria, the editor has published such articles as:

"A New Church in an Old Style"—the story of Trinity Episcopal Church at Upperville, Virginia, a building compared architecturally to the Gothic cathedrals of Europe.

"Crossing the River at White's Ferry"—an article telling of a picturesque ferry over the Potomac in Montgomery County, Maryland.

And, in the unusual person category, *Sunday* published an article entitled "Grandmas of the Rails" about two Maryland grandmothers who operate a "speeder" in the B & O yards at Brunswick, Maryland.

What should you write for your Sunday supplement? Your material should be timely and definitely local in subject matter. If your town has solved a problem of juvenile delinquency, has a "rock hound" who has become a skillful gem cutter, or has a resident who is a noted author or artist, probably your Sunday supplement would be glad to see an article on this subject.

Most of the supplements buy both text and photographs for illustrations. Your pay, therefore, may range from $25 to $100 or perhaps more for an illustrated feature. This is a market well worth your best efforts. You may use it as a stepping stone to the big national supplements such as the *Family Weekly, Parade* and *This Week—* publications which pay handsomely for acceptable copy.

Just what do the big national supplements want in the way of material and what restrictions do they place on submissions? Here are valuable guidelines from John O'Connell, former editor of *This Week:*

Editors of Sunday supplements have generally learned to endure the difficulties of working with small space for editorial content and, in my opinion, the situation may be a blessing in disguise. Why? Because today, many magazines proceed on the principle that their first editorial problem is the brevity of the material offered.

One famous weekly, for instance, recently ran an article of some 20,000 words on the deplorable condition of State governments. A Manhattan supplement got equally lavish in its treatment of Mayor Lindsay and other local phenomena of presumably absorbing interest.

I don't go along with this thinking as applied in those cases, and far less so for a publication as attenuated as *This Week*. When people go in for a lengthy bout of reading, the object usually is not a general magazine but a book or, in special cases, something to do with their work. In other words, I think people turn to general magazines for just a smattering of the subject—enough to give them something to talk about.

In the regular features in *This Week,* we try to convey information briefly and entertainingly. Even the lead and secondary articles are presented to attract not only the person who may be interested enough in the subject to spend a little time with it, but also for the scanner, a class to which most of today's readers belong. This method of presentation, I feel, is in tune with the times.

Television has something to do with it. Watching TV, we have grown used to constant interruptions. If they are not forced on us by commercials, cuts and so on, we invite them by getting up to spin the dial in search for something more entertaining. As a consequence, our span of attention has been shortened. We grow impatient with long-drawn-out things more quickly than we used to. Have you lately watched a child try to read a book?

But it isn't only TV. The arts are suffering a kind of fragmentation. Music has grown episodic and discordant; in painting and sculpture, there has been a deliberate breaking up of form. In movies, it's often difficult to tell what's happening. Audiences today, right or wrong, no longer pay as close attention to motivations and complications, cause and effect, as they did in calmer days.

Most people don't have the time for all this and I believe they resent it when magazine editors insist they do have, and foist on them subjects that assume interests and habits the reader simply doesn't possess any more. Therefore, at *This Week,* we have been sharpening —fragmenting—our features.

The problem of the first editorial page is always knotty. Our "Headliner Interview" is based on two notions: (1) People are more interesting than anything; and (2) "name" people are usually more interesting than anonymous ones, and generally say more interesting things.

On Easter Sunday, a day when people supposedly don't read or respond, we ran a cover of a Korean child and a Headliner Interview with Dr. Howard Rusk, director of the American-Korean Founda-

This Week

MAGAZINE

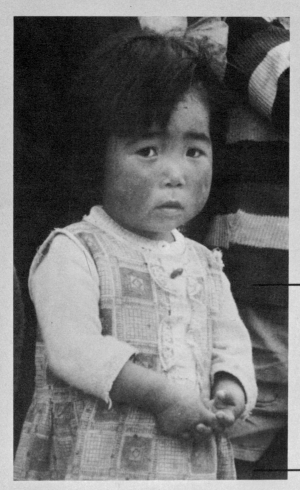

HOW YOU BECAME
WHAT YOU ARE

*New research with identical
twins tells a great deal more
about heredity and environment*

PAGE 4

*Six Frenchmen Take a Voyage
to the Bottom of the Sea*

PAGE 12

PLUS: *People in Action, Food,
Great Ideas and The Odd One*

A special
Easter
thought

*You can buy a house for this
homeless Korean child and her
family — cost: $150*

PAGE 2

tion. He informed our readers that a house could be built for a home-less Korean family for only $150. More than 300 homes have been purchased by our readers and the Foundation, based on these re-turns, is beginning the construction of several villages.

As for lead articles, we ran one by Senator Edward Kennedy about the need for drastic changes in the draft law. Anyone who has anyone affected by the draft, which is almost everyone, read this. It was the longest article in the issue, but still ran to only 2,000 words.

We believe, then, in this editorial approach for *This Week,* with the exception of the sporadic "Keepsake Issues" which cover a single subject. Parenthetically, the "Keepsakes," too, lend themselves to this approach, because the first of these was our immigration issue, titled "The Golden Door," which drew great reader response. We published another "Keepsake" devoted to baseball and it attracted so much attention that it was praised over television and radio by commentators.

We also try to talk directly to young people. The success we have had with "Zipcode"—a teenage information exchange column—has encouraged us to think we have our foot in the door to that vast audience.

For writers, the best approach to *This Week* is through a query, especially about articles. A query gives an editor a chance to use his rules, and a chance to get in on the act at the start. Queried properly, invited to participate, he can tell you all about his magazine, what it wants and doesn't want.

That great basic principle, "The More You Work at Something, the More You Grow to Love It" goes into operation. If the editor is given a chance to work on your article, he's going to wind up loving it almost as much as you do.

Well, what makes a good query? First, it is brief and . . .

a. Gives the essential facts;
b. Suggests why these facts should be interesting to the reader, and finally—
c. Mentions how the writer is going to treat them.

The purpose of the query, remember, is simply to interest the edi-tor. If he wants to know more, he may ask for an outline. That would be good news indeed for the writer, because at least half the ideas that go into most magazines develop at conferences.

Whom can we get to do a crime piece, a tax piece, a medical piece? Instantly, a number of names suggest themselves, names of writers who specialize in these fields. As a result, the editor doesn't have to experiment with writers who may not be able to give him what he wants.

At *This Week,* we have become more and more dedicated to the principle that lead stories must be conversation pieces. I don't mean the exposé sort of thing, more suited to newsstand magazines than to a supplement appearing in many papers with many different editorial views. I don't even mean being controversial. I mean articles which say things of which the reader was already vaguely aware but never before quite appreciated.

A good example of this was our career-wife-housewife battle, titled "Other Women Hate Me." We ran the career wife's side of the story and got so much irate mail that we were happily forced into a follow-up piece, giving the housewife's views.

This might have been predicted, but when we ran the first story, we didn't plan a playback. What we were looking for was a single article to draw heavy reader response. Always we try to excite, entertain and inform readers Sunday-after-Sunday. This requires new thinking every week, and I suggest that many would-be writers would surely make it if they also thought in the same terms.

Before we leave the field of journalism, local or Sunday, let's look at still another area of newspaper work not as remote from the average writer as it might appear. In the following article, written by Dorothy Kostka for the *Famous Writers Magazine,* a successful woman writer tells how she got into the column business and gives helpful suggestions for others who would like to follow in her footsteps:

Nearly every writer cherishes a secret longing to be a columnist. It looks so ridiculously easy. All the columnist does is sit at his typewriter and knock out a few hundred words of personal opinion. Not for him the painstaking research involved in article writing or the exhausting struggle with a stubborn fiction plot. He's syndicated, he reaches an audience of millions—*and* he makes pots of money!

We may forget, as we read a columnist, that behind this writing lies special knowledge and competence in some field or experience acquired over years of living. This is why he's qualified to write a column. He has something substantial to say concerning a subject about which he knows quite a lot.

Perhaps this is true of you, too, and if you can bring to your special knowledge a fresh slant and an engaging style, you have a good chance to break into the column-writing field. This market is close at hand, right outside your front door where the boy drops the weekly or daily newspaper. If you live in a small town, it's probably a weekly and you know the editor personally. These weeklies (6,315 of them in our country) offer a splendid opportunity to the new writer who hasn't made a name for himself. Your hopeful goal is syndication, but you must be published first, and your best bet is a local editor who can be persuaded to give your column a trial.

Let's consider your qualifications for column writing. For your own sake, you should be a facile writer. Words must come to you fairly easily or the agony you'll undergo as you try to keep your column going won't be worth it. You should write thoughtfully, responsibly and as well as you can, but with an awareness that you're not writing for the ages. For the editor's sake, you should be a disciplined writer. He's saving space for you and he has a deadline he expects you to meet. If you fail him, you'll shortly be an ex-columnist.

I'm now in the third year of writing a column called "Freedom after Fifty" for the Denver *Post*. It's published on Sunday in "Contemporary"—the women's magazine section. My columns are longish, 500 words or a little more, and are more suitable for weekly use.

Freedom after FIFTY

By DOROTHY KOSTKA

LET'S CONSIDER the follies of middle-aged and elderly men.

Mr. and Mrs. S. had enjoyed Sunday dinner with their daughter and son-in-law as usual. Then the son-in-law left to attend a meeting and Mr. S. went out to warm up his car.

a 100-year-old man, who still worked at his factory job four hours a day. Mr. R., who'd stopped working at 65, was feeling a little inferior.

THE SNOW WAS wet and heavy on the shovel. Mr. R. was soon panting in the thin, mile-high air. At his last check-up had inquired

During the first week of each month I write my columns for the following month. I write two, sometimes three in one day from ideas I've tucked away in my file. As I begin each column, I jot down the points I want to make in their logical sequence. Then I think for a while about the style I should use in this particular column.

I write for the middle-aged and the elderly from an optimistic, buoyant "let's-enjoy-these-years" viewpoint. Some columns are factual, dealing with such subjects as retirement, health, recreation, employment. These are usually written in a straight article style.

However, people over fifty are, or should be, still involved in the world. We have relationships with younger people. We have personal problems and personal needs. We hope, we doubt, we suffer, we make mistakes. In these areas, my column offers my own philosophy on how to remain loving and lovable human beings all our lives. I sometimes present this philosophy in a fictional form, using characters, setting and conversation. These changes in technique help to keep my column varied and alive. In all my columns, I permit my personality, my experiences and my opinions to flavor my writing.

We'll assume that you're facile and disciplined but can you *communicate?* In our big and indifferent world, people are increasingly hungry for warm contact with others. You must "come alive" to your readers as a real person. Often I meet a stranger who will say, "Oh, you're Dorothy Kostka! I feel as though I *know* you."

Sometimes I achieve reader-identification. Not long ago a friend said: "You write the things I've always thought and didn't know how to say." This quality is essential in a personal column and it's useful even in factual writing. If someone feels that he "knows" you and is interested in your ideas, you've acquired a loyal reader.

The subject matter of your column will depend on what you know and what you feel is important to communicate to others. This list is almost endless. In factual writing: household hints, cooking, sewing, knitting, hobbies, pets, etiquette, gardening, health, finance, politics, bridge, beauty tips, literature, music, art. Personal columns include: marriage problems, child care, parent-child relationships, the teen-ager, older people, religion, humor, the kind of column that began with "Dear Dorothy Dix" and now is flourishing as "Dear Abby," and the general "This-is-what-I-think" column.

Consider your own experiences in living, which may qualify you to help others with your hard-won knowledge. If you're well known in a small community, people may want to read your column simply because you're *you.*

I chose to write a personal advice column for people over fifty for two reasons. I'd reached that age myself and discovered that the later years hold many rich rewards. Surely, I reasoned, there were others like myself who'd welcome a reinforcement of their feelings of personal worth and their zest for living. I might also be helpful to some who had bogged down in self-pity and useless longing for the past.

The second reason concerned my writing career. Although I'm primarily a fiction writer, I began to write "art-of-living" articles a long time ago. So long ago, in fact, that my first such piece dealt with the etiquette of pregnancy and was titled, "Don't Make *Him* Have That Baby!" Articles on family relationships and social problems followed, so I was accustomed to reaching my reader on a personal basis and in a counseling role.

Now, let's sell your column. You don't begin by approaching an editor with the bare bones of your idea. Outline what you plan to do and then write about a dozen sample columns. My own sample columns were written on the general subjects of the health, personality and opportunities for personal fulfillment of the woman over fifty. I called it "Women after Fifty" but the editor changed it to "Freedom after Fifty." This was wise, because my column is read by many men. Hold your column to 500 words at a maximum. Newspapers never have enough space—except for ads.

Prepare a sales talk about your audience and what you can offer them. I knew how many people over fifty were living in our country and something about their interests and their problems. Gardening? Look into your local garden clubs, their activities and membership. Children? Cooking? Everyone has children and everyone cooks, but you might want to know about school dropouts and juvenile delinquency in your area or the circulation of cookbooks at your library and the status of home economics instruction in your schools. You must exercise your own ingenuity.

Take your sample columns and your sales talk to the newspaper that you think offers you the best chance to break into print. As I suggested before, a weekly newspaper can be a good springboard. However, there's no reason to shy away from a daily—big or small. Your problem here may be competition from a syndicated column in your field. Don't let that frighten you. If you can write a better column, he's out and you're in.

I live in a suburb of Denver, with two weekly newspapers, but I didn't submit my column to those outlets because I'd written many articles for the Denver *Post* and had contacts on that newspaper. The *Post* was using at the time a syndicated retirement column that seemed to me to be stale and repetitious. It was dropped a few weeks after my column started.

After your column has taken hold, you will want to extend its publication. If you're being published in a weekly or daily that circulates in a limited area, you can reach out to other newspapers in the state. Send them half a dozen tear sheets, with a covering letter. In the case of a large daily, such as the Denver *Post*, I'm not free to do this because it's circulated all over the state of Colorado and in a half a dozen neighboring states.

Syndication is a beautiful goal and one worth striving for. I must be honest and explain that it's crowded. The syndicate directory issued by *Editor and Publisher* lists over 40 syndicates that carry about 1,600 columns on every imaginable subject. Syndicate editors are busy, they're rushed, they have a backlog of columns waiting to be launched.

I wasn't daunted by these facts, nor should you be. I selected eight top syndicates and sent them tear sheets with a covering letter. They all read my columns, I'm convinced, and a writer can't ask for more. Their letters were flattering but that blasted backlog kept cropping up. I haven't given up hope of syndication. Sometime the lightning may strike me—or *you!*

Now your column's launched and you must keep it going. When I first started writing "Freedom after Fifty," my husband observed: "You're going to be the Abby Van Buren of the wheelchair set."

I wasn't a bit ruffled. "That'll be fine," I said, but I was speaking from the depths of ignorance. I was visualizing all those people over fifty writing in to ask me to solve their problems. All that would be required were a few sage words of advice.

I failed to realize that people over fifty are like *me*. We don't ask for advice. We give it. My fan mail consists principally of comments on my column, written as one friend would write to another. I acknowledge every one. The elderly are often lonely people. Sometimes they phone me, just to chat. As I was working on this article, an elderly man called. I listened to him patiently and my reward was his remark, "You write as though it comes from your heart."

Sometimes a reader wants to share with me a sorrow or a joy. A woman wrote me about her daughter-in-law who seemed to "slam the door" on her, and this germinated a column on this often-difficult relationship. Another letter described happy retirement in a mobile home and I used an excerpt in a column on this subject. Occasionally there are questions such as: "How can three generations live in harmony under one roof?" and "Should I marry a middle-aged bachelor with a possessive mother?"

My experiences in living account for some columns. Examples are: my thoughts on what we owe our adult children and what we shouldn't give them; the fears of the later years; the folly of regret; the bad habits of the "middle-aged marriage" or the problems of loneliness.

Reading and research are often required. For a two-part piece on jobs for older women, I took a three-hour vocational aptitude test and interviewed job counselors. I researched my facts for columns on Social Security and Medicare, the different kinds of retirement facilities, the technique of will-making, inheritance taxes, financial facts for wives. I took a hearing test and wrote columns on deafness and hearing aids. I interviewed three older women who had returned to college, and wrote about this new trend.

"I researched my facts for columns on Social Security and Medicare . . ."

My best source of all is what I hear, see and read. Once you're in the groove with your column, you become highly sensitive to everything that's related to your subject. For instance, I heard two grandmothers talking on a bus. One said to her friend, "I adore having our grandchildren visit us but I'm glad to see them go, too. That's natural, I hope." Her friend assured her it was, but I detected a guilty note in their voices. I wrote a column on "the new breed of grandmothers" as opposed to the "cookie-jar grandma."

A friend in his sixties fell off a stepladder while cleaning rain gutters, broke his arm and shattered his knee. This inspired a column on the foolish things older men do, including pushing stalled cars and shoveling snow. I heard a woman say, "I won't let Jim retire. He'd drive me crazy, sitting around the house all day." I came up with some ideas on happy (or at least tolerable) 24-hour togetherness for the retired couple.

"She's crawled in a shell and won't come out for anyone," a woman observed about her widowed sister-in-law. I talked to several widowed friends and wrote a column suggesting practical ways of adjusting to the loss of a husband. A beautiful woman in her fifties, who tells her age without the quiver of an eyelash, talked to me about "the richness of the past" and how much it adds to our enjoyment of the present, if we don't deny it. I used her thoughts in a column.

I wrote in short-story form the experience of a retired couple, who pulled up their lifelong roots and went to California to be near their only child. In three months they were back, admitting it had been a mistake. Watching a TV interview with a cosmetic surgeon spawned a column on the desperate means to which some women resort to keep their youth.

I have a file of newspaper and magazine clippings and one-sentence notes I've written to myself under the general headings of appearance, finances, health, jobs, personality, recreation, relatives, retirement. In planning each month's column, I try to keep a balance between fact and philosophy.

Unless you're capable of this sustained effort, your column may be short-lived. During my time on the Denver *Post*, I've seen this happen to several promising new columns. One was called "You and Your Child" and was written by a psychiatrist. He invited questions from readers and while waiting for them wrote an erudite, rather dull column on this lively and provocative subject. The letters didn't materialize and the column soon disappeared.

If you fail to become syndicated, the financial return for writing a column won't be large. I had an amusing hassle with the woman's editor of the *Post* (who happens to be a man) when we came to the sticky subject of payment. He pointed out plaintively that the paper pays an average of $7.50 for a syndicated column. I pointed out, also plaintively, that my column was exclusive with the *Post*. We reached a figure that doesn't compensate me for the time involved but I still have those syndication stars in my eyes.

If you can syndicate your column and sell it to 75 or 100 papers at $7.50 each per week, less the syndicate commission, you'll have a tidy income. There's also the possibility of publishing your columns in book form. I've now written about 90,000 words on the subject of successful living in the later years and I plan to select, edit and re-arrange this material for book publication.

Personal rewards that won't show in your bank balance will come your way. Column writing is a marvelous ego-builder and every writer, even the most successful, needs constant reassurance that he can write something worthy of publication and payment. You'll also have the satisfaction of knowing that you are reaching other people with your knowledge and your values, advising or influencing them, clarifying their thinking or helping them in practical ways to live more happily and fully.

You'll be given many opportunities to speak to groups. Readers of your column will be curious about you, eager to meet you in person and see for themselves what you're "really like." I feel an obligation to do this and I find it's great fun. The subject of your talk, of course, depends on the nature of your column.

My present talk, which is on the light side, is called "The Seven Ages of Woman." It expresses my sincere belief that women are the fortunate sex, should realize this and stop pushing. Both men and women seem to enjoy my talk. And don't be too hasty in saying, "I don't charge anything." Many small groups can't pay, but others will if you hesitate long enough for them to make an offer.

If you want to try a column, dig deep into your mind, identify your interests and capabilities, evaluate your knowledge and experience. Then choose the subject that you'll enjoy writing about.

The market for juvenile material

Another good place for the writer to break into print is the juvenile magazine field. For one thing, there are many of these publications—approximately 500. (There are only 30 publications in the field of general editorial magazines such as *Life, Saturday Evening Post, Look,* and *Reader's Digest.*) The pay scale ranges from good to poor, but with so many outlets looking for material, requirements aren't as high as those of the big magazines. However, don't get the idea that since standards are lower, requirements are not definite. Each of these magazines is designed for a specific audience and the editors won't accept anything that doesn't meet requirements. Don't simply "write

Juvenile magazines often provide the new writer with his first opportunity to break into print.

something for kids" and then attempt to find an editor who will buy it. Study your market and slant your piece accordingly.

The juvenile magazines operate under a special set of rules. To begin with, most of them are not published to make money; many are produced by church and religious organizations. Their aim is to uplift and instruct. Unless your story contains some kind of "message" an editor wants to get across, you are not likely to make a sale.

Further, each juvenile magazine is aimed at a definite age group. An article on human relations for *Ingenue,* a magazine for teen-age girls, isn't going to appeal to the staff of *Highlights for Children,* written for children between three and twelve.

Even the requirements within the same age group vary greatly. The emphasis in *Nature and Science,* published by the Museum of Natural History for ages nine to fourteen is different from the emphasis you'll find in *News Explorer* or *Newstime* put out by Scholastic Magazines for children ages nine to ten and eleven to twelve. Each publication is aimed at a certain audience and unless you shape your contribution to this aim, your chances of success are poor indeed.

Since the field is at once so large and so limited, your best bet is to consult an up-to-date market list and evaluate the juvenile publications. Go through this list and pick out half a dozen or so that seem to publish the sort of thing you can write; then get hold of several copies of each, from your library's back-number shelves, from a back-number bookstore or direct from the publishers.

However, since the requirements of one magazine may be similar but not identical to those of another in the same field, we suggest you prepare an analysis sheet—one for each magazine you want to contact. Something like this would do:

Magazine: ....

Address: ....

Editor: ....

To whom does magazine appeal? Type of reader, age group?
Editorial policies? Slant of articles. Teach? Amuse? Taboos.
Standards? Length of articles, rates of pay, payment on acceptance, publication? Use of photographs, color?
Style? Formal, informal, colorful.
Types of article? (Describe briefly, with titles, several articles of type you think you can do.)

You may hesitate to prepare such sheets because of the time involved, but don't forget that the effort can save you much time in the long run. You could use such a sheet three times in selling one article to one magazine: once when preparing your query; again when preparing your working outline; and third, as a final check before submitting the finished manuscript.

One advantage of writing for the juveniles, which partially offsets the average low pay, is that competition isn't as strong as in the higher pay fields. Further, if you show possibilities as a contributor, editors will work with you to a generous extent.

Another point in favor of the juveniles is the excellent training offered. Many of today's highest paid non-fiction writers started as writers for young readers.

Selling to the religious magazines

The religious magazine field is even larger than the juvenile in point of magazines published. What we have just said about the magazines in the young people's group applies even more directly to the religious area. While a number of them simply stress "Christian principles," with no sectarian limitation, roughly two-thirds are printed by various church groups, with the consequent requirement of harmonious treatment in the articles. By far the largest single group is Catholic—about a third of all religious magazines published.

Our suggestion about surveying a magazine field first, then narrowing your choice to half a dozen for rigorous study, applies even more sharply here. Your library will probably not carry many religious magazines and the back-number stores won't, either. So the simplest solution is write to the publishers and ask for sample copies. If you enclose ten cents to cover handling and mailing, your thoughtfulness will be appreciated; many religious magazines operate on a limited budget.

Generally speaking, the religious editors are the most helpful of all. If you show possibilities as a contributor, you'll receive warm cooperation, a worthwhile fee and find yourself in print more quickly than by almost any other route.

Preparing fillers and shorts

First, what *are* fillers and shorts? Bennett Cerf describes them this way:

Since almost no article comes out exactly the right size, every page of a magazine issue presents a make-up problem. About an inch to three inches of blank space must be filled with something. Thus, the mathematics of printing creates a market for the novice writer, offering him a chance of breaking into print through the filler and the short, and giving him his first cash sale.

Because the primary function of a filler or short is to fill out a page or column, it obviously need not have anything to do with the material it follows. For a good example of a newspaper filler, here's a column from *The New York Times*. The item about a lost ship was too short to fill the space to the top of an ad, so a brief but interesting item about a fire was inserted. If this one hadn't fitted, the make-up man had others of different lengths to choose from.

LOST SHIP'S MASTER DESCRIBES DAMAGE

The master of the Canadian freighter Charny said yesterday that he ordered his crew to abandon the vessel in the Atlantic last Friday when he discovered the ship's pumps could no longer keep up with leakage on the port side.

"The ship was listing 30 degrees, and the situation was dangerous," Capt. Joels Jourdai of Rimouski, Quebec, said yesterday during a stop at Kennedy International Airport.

The ship sank Sunday about 520 miles off Cape Hatteras, N. C., after being taken under tow by a tugboat.

The ship's master said the freighter apparently had developed a crack in the hull after running into a storm. The ship was carrying a cargo of pipes and water-pumping equipment to Bermuda.

Commenting on the efforts of United States Air Force and Coast Guard rescue planes, which dropped life rafts to the group, the 41-year-old master said, "They did a marvelous job. They were really in charge of the situation."

Fire Imperils Constellation

BALTIMORE, Feb. 12 (AP)— Flames destroyed a lumber warehouse, several automobiles and a number of tractor trailers and for a while threatened the United States frigate Constellation tonight on Baltimore's waterfront. The frigate, launched in Baltimore in 1797, was not damaged. She is now a tourist attraction.

Most newspapers and magazines use fillers—another good outlet for beginning writers.

The supplying of shorts and fillers offers a good market to beginning writers. Virtually all magazines use them and the pay is quite good in terms of the time involved in preparation. Naturally, the items fall into certain categories: quotable quotes, bits of humor, bright sayings of children, unusual anecdotes, picturesque speech, eavesdropping, wry comments on the passing scene—brief items which delight the compositor.

Another type of filler is the *departmental short*. These include: household hints, recipes, letters to the magazine, contributions to regular monthly features which earn the sender a few dollars and display his name. Some magazines have a large staff which does nothing but cull the world of print for shorts and fillers. The *New Yorker,* for instance, is famous for reprinting newspaper paragraphs containing typographical errors, transposed lines and mixed metaphors. The editors of this department reach heights of humor in comments printed under such headlines as "Department of Utter Confusion," "Funny Coincidence Department," "Mixed Metaphor Department" or "Department of Oversimplification."

Another filler to consider is the household hint. Have you worked out a simple way of opening screwtop jars when they're stuck? Do you have a friend who has invented a quick way of cleaning paint brushes? What about that neighbor with the novel method of collecting fallen leaves in the autumn? Any improved way of doing a common household task quicker or better is almost a sure sale on the filler market, as long as it's short, simple—and works. Example:

Next time you use a paint roller, line the tray with aluminum foil. When you're through, throw the foil liner away. This saves the messy job of cleaning the tray.

Where do you sell shorts and fillers? There are literally thousands of markets in the United States, many of them trade journals, homecraft or regional publications, or Sunday editions of big newspapers. The elementary short constantly used in such publications is a good place for the beginning writer to break into print because:

1. The style of each publication is easy to follow.
2. Every writer has items from his own knowledge that no one else is likely to contribute.

3. Friends and relatives add to his source material constantly, if he keeps his ears open.

4. A writer can often find in one publication an item that can easily be rewritten or adapted for another.

5. Acceptable shorts and fillers, when contributed to the same magazine over a long period, often lead to writing assignments from the editor.

In *Article Writing and Marketing,* George L. Bird points out that the general style of the short item is much the same as that of longer articles:

It should be free from useless words and sentences. Extra-careful pruning will eliminate what is unnecessary. When editing these items, ask what is accomplished by each word or by each sentence. If the sentence element is not important, try leaving it out. Sentences and paragraphs should be shorter, perhaps, than in long articles. The sentences are terse and exact—to the point.

The *first sentence must state the main idea to be explained or illustrated.* Later sentences merely add the details or make specific applications. If the item consists of a single sentence, make the first five words or the first line give the gist of the idea.

Avoid long words and technical words, unless they are explained. Use the common, everyday words on the tongue of everyone. Because the result will be good English, it will most likely be understood by the mass of readers. Here's an example of the topic sentence, followed by an explanatory statement:

(a) Beads are restrung more easily when placed on corrugated cardboard or a piece of pleated material.

(b) This prevents them from rolling around and getting mixed up as to size or position.

You can write the lead on a short in many ways, but the more condensed and precise a short is, the more an editor will like it. Magazines don't pay by the word for shorts and fillers, as they often do for longer articles. There's usually a standard price, say $10 to $100, for each item accepted, regardless of length.

Let's try another short formula of (a) a topic sentence, then (b) a statement of how the reader would follow the routine or the advice you give:

(a) An ordinary pocketknife makes a good candleholder when no other is available.

(b) Open the knife with the large blade fully extended. The small blade should be half extended. Thrust the large blade into a tree trunk, tent pole or other upright, with the small blade straight up, at right angles to the big blade. Push the candle down upon the point of the small upright blade.

Both the foregoing examples of shorts were written by beginning writers and sold to *Popular Mechanics* and *Popular Science*, which print hundreds of such items annually. In each case the items appeared under departmental headings of "how to do it more easily." The writers had no special training, but they did possess alert minds: they cashed in on their wits. They had experienced or been told of the tricks for restringing beads and using a pocketknife as a candleholder.

The filler area is so vast that its full definition must be left to your observation of individual magazines. Styles and requirements change. But two things are constant in writing and marketing shorts and fillers:

1. They must be special.
2. They must be succinct.

By special, we mean provocative, dramatic, humorous, touching, moving, highly informative, even tricky, besides being tightly, sparsely written. Many shorts and fillers have a twist, frequently at the end. Sometimes they resemble the old-fashioned two-line joke where the first sentence sets up the situation and the second sentence gives it just enough of a twist to cause you to laugh, make you say to yourself: "Why didn't I think of that?"

Instant research

Writers who subscribe to the *Reader's Digest* and keep the issues for possible reference will be interested to know about an "instant-research" method allowing them to look up any previously published *Digest* article. The genie is an annual *Reader's Digest Index*, available free to all writers. You simply write the *Digest* at Pleasantville, N.Y., tell them you are a professional writer and ask to be put on their *Index* mailing list. They'll be glad to send you the *Index* at the end of every year.—Mort Weisinger in *A Treasury of Tips for Writers*

Section IX

Lesson fifteen

Special markets

Part II

In this, the second Lesson devoted to special markets, we take up still other areas which carry on the teaching in Lesson Fourteen. Among these additional markets is one bearing the general heading "Nature." Here is a subject all around us in the world where we live—a subject as inexhaustible in content as in scope. Yet for some reason, perhaps because of its very familiarity, most writers seldom think about it. However, the requirements are very simple: you need eyes to see, patience to observe and a pencil and notebook to record observations.

Nature in its various forms is ever-present—in the green of spring grass, the burgeoning trees and shrubs, the insect, animal and bird life, the clouds. And each season has its own activities and interests. Countless untold stories lie close at hand, just waiting for the observer to see them and the imaginative mind to run them through the typewriter for others to enjoy.

The best-selling author Edwin Way Teale wrote of "wildlife" in his backyard and an adjoining apple orchard. He studied the insects that abounded there, photographed them, learned all he could about them. The result was one of his first major books, *Grassroot Jungles*. Five years later, he followed with *Near*

Horizons, subtitled "The Story of an Insect Garden." The material for both these books, which did much to establish him as one of the world's foremost nature writers, literally came from his own backyard.

Going further afield, Teale came up with a series of four books, each dealing with one season. Each volume required extensive research, since this author is no armchair naturalist. With his wife he drove to the tip of Florida; then they worked their way *North with the Spring,* the title of this first volume in *The American Seasons* series. Published in 1951, some nine years after Teale first broached the idea to his publisher, it included material gleaned from 17,000 miles of driving, the taking of thousands of photographs and the keeping of voluminous notes which he completed at the end of each day.

The series was completed in 1965—some 22 years after inception—with *Wandering through Winter,* which won the Pulitzer Prize for general non-fiction. And between these volumes Teale researched and wrote *Autumn across America* and *Journey into Summer,* along with several lesser projects. The *Seasons* books, the distillation of his research, represent more than 100,000 miles of driving.

Not many writers are situated so they can devote years to such a project, but Teale's experience points up what can be done by a dedicated naturalist who also is an accomplished writer. When asked for a few words of advice to aspiring nature writers, he said:

It's easy to be interesting and inaccurate. It's easy to be accurate and dull. But to be both interesting *and* accurate is the great goal. And that is a goal that takes a considerable amount of work to achieve.

No discussion of nature writing would be complete without mention of Henry David Thoreau (1817-1862) and John Muir (1838-1914). Stalwart pioneers in the nature writing field, their works are classics. Though Thoreau died more than a century ago, the latest edition of *Books in Print* lists almost a column of his titles in various editions.

As for John Muir, his works live as a literary monument to his efforts to make America aware of the importance of conservation. He spent most of his life getting close to nature and his field trips on foot led him on treks up to 1,000 miles. No outburst of nature could keep him from enjoying the beauties and the strengths of the elements. This is how he described an experience in *The Mountains of California:*

Naturalist John Muir and Theodore Roosevelt survey California's Yosemite Valley from the summit of Glacier Point.

One of the most beautiful and exhilarating storms I ever enjoyed in the Sierra occurred in December, 1874, when I happened to be exploring one of the tributary valleys of the Yuba River. The sky and the ground and the trees had been thoroughly rain-washed and were dry again. The day was intensely pure, one of those incomparable bits of California winter, warm and balmy and full of white sparkling sunshine, redolent of all the purest influences of the spring, and at the same time enlivened with one of the most bracing wind-storms conceivable.

Instead of camping out, as I usually do, I then chanced to be stopping at the house of a friend. But when the storm began to sound, I lost no time in pushing out into the woods to enjoy it. For on such occasions Nature has always something rare to show us, and the danger to life and limb is hardly greater than one would experience crouching deprecatingly beneath a roof. . . .

I heard trees falling for hours at the rate of one every two or three minutes; some uprooted, partly on account of the loose, water-soaked condition of the ground; others broken straight across, where some weakness caused by fire had determined the spot. The gestures of the trees made a delightful study. Young sugar pines, light and feathery as squirrel-tails, were bowing almost to the ground; while the grand old patriarchs, whose massive boles had been tried in a hundred storms waved solemnly above them, their long, arching branches streaming fluently in the gale, and every needle thrilling and ringing and shedding off keen lances of light like a diamond. . . . But the silver pines were now the most impressively beautiful of all. Colossal spires 200 feet in height waved like supple goldenrods chanting and bowing as if in worship, while the whole mass of their long, tremulous foliage was kindled into one continuous blaze of white sun-fire. The force of the gale was such that the steadfast monarch of them all rocked down to its roots with a motion plainly perceptible when one leaned against it. Nature was holding high festival, and every fiber of the most rigid giants thrilled with glad excitement.

Any reader will agree that there's imagination in Muir's writing and, while imagination is stressed as one of the prime requisites of fiction, it's equally important in non-fiction.

Imagination is a powerful tool

As a further example of using imagination to present a nature subject, consider how Paul and Myriam Friggens introduced their experiences in America's national park, Canyonlands. Here's their lead as it appeared in *Reader's Digest* under the title "Standing-up Country":

Halting our pack outfit on a canyon rim, we gazed in awe at America's newest national park. Before us towered battlements resembling some medieval fortress or fairy-tale castle; sandstone skyscrapers that might have been the Manhattan skyline; spires and needles higher than the Washington Monument. Here the Colorado River and the Green, while slicing through stair-stepped plateaus and down-plunging canyons, had laid bare 200 million years of geologic history in colorful 3-D.

It's "standing-up country" ('There's more of it standing up than laying down!' an old-time cowpuncher described it) and probably the greatest red-rock fantasy on earth. Officially, the new park is called Canyonlands.

Immediately the reader can visualize this colorful country and is eager to learn more about it. Why? Because the writers brought a bit of imagination to the subject.

Beginning non-fiction writers, taking material close at hand, often write about their pets. One trouble here is that many people aren't able to distinguish between material interesting to them and that which has wide general appeal. Our own pets are something special to us, but they're a good deal like our children—other folks don't always think they're cute.

Sterling North, however, wrote a book about his boyhood experiences with a young raccoon and the volume became a best seller. Though it is a simple story of a boy and his pet, it has universal appeal. *Rascal,* the name of the coon and the book, was a real character, and the account is full of interesting happenings, complete with suspense and drama. So, as you consider nature writing, be sure your material has broad human interest. If it doesn't, no editor will consider it.

You never know when or where you'll come upon a nature subject worth at least a newspaper feature. New York newspapers not long ago had stories about a porcupine strolling along a busy street in lower Manhattan. Finally it was captured and hustled off to a shelter by men from the SPCA.

The publications that use nature stories are many and varied. They range all the way from the *Reader's Digest* to magazines devoted to pets, and include livestock journals, outdoor magazines, and even children's magazines. And don't overlook the Sunday supplements and the travel sections. Just keep in mind that the story you tackle must have strong human interest and that it must be told well.

The aspiring writer of nature stories who lives in the country or in a small town may have an advantage over the city dweller, for there's more to see. However, this didn't deter John Kieran. A long-time resident of New York, a sports writer and a radio and television personality, he is also a student of nature. Realizing that few New Yorkers were aware of the great variety of wildlife to be found within the city limits, he decided to inform them. The result was *A Natural History of New York*. Through the years his other nature books, including *Footnotes on Na-*

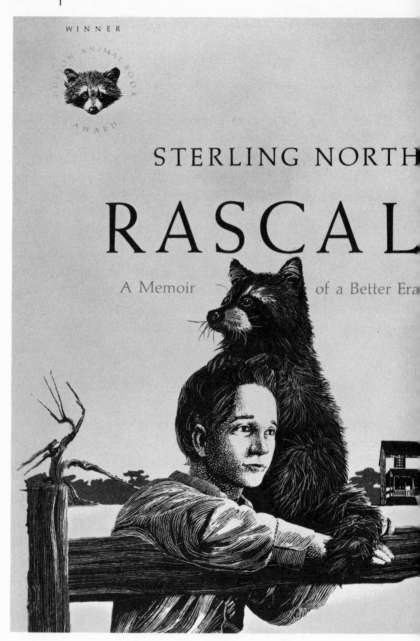

WINNER

STERLING NORTH

RASCAL

A Memoir   of a Better Era

The dust jacket of Sterling North's best seller about his boyhood experiences with a young raccoon.

ture, An Introduction to Wild Flowers and *An Introduction to Nature,* have entertained and informed countless readers.

So, if you have an observing eye and a receptive ear, a keen interest in the subject, and the ability to use a little imagination in presenting your material, nature provides an inexhaustible source for articles and books, regardless of where you live. What are you waiting for?

Writing about outdoor sports

Outdoors writing is an area where the author cannot depend on libraries or interviews; it is a first-person field. You have to go to the place and do the things you want to write about. If the outdoors writer is writing about deer hunting, he must know what he's talking about and know it well—the same with any other sports subject where you can get in trouble unless you know what you're doing. Yet, many writers who like hunting or hiking, fishing or camping, have been spending years building up a salable background of expert knowledge without realizing it. Now they have a chance to cash in. Next time you go on a fishing trip, pack a notebook with your tackle box. You may come back with an article that will pay for the whole expedition.

The outdoors writer must be able to take his reader by the hand, make him share the thrill of landing a giant sailfish, of stalking a shy and wary animal, of studying a rare bird. The ability to let your reader watch over your shoulder is the basic necessity of this form of writing. If you don't have it, the article simply won't come off. If you do have it, you have a very valuable skill. And like many other skills, it improves with practice.

Supplying pictures with your text

Any outdoors piece should lean strongly on illustration. Here's what a successful outdoors writer, Ted Wachs, a former instructor at the Famous Writers School, has to say about furnishing visual material. In the *Famous Writers Magazine,* he talked about supplying photos for fishing and hunting articles:

At first I thought (and why not?) that my inspired prose had sold the story on lake-trout fishing at Lincoln Pond. But when the next issue of *Fishing World* came out, I knew the truth as soon as I opened the pages: without photographs I wouldn't have had a salable piece.

In camera close-ups, the few middling-sized trout we caught took on noble proportions. And the view of Lincoln Pond, mirroring the mountains and shoreline spruce trees, went far beyond my powers to describe in words the quiet splendor of the Maine woods.

"And the view of Lincoln Pond, mirroring the mountains and shoreline spruce trees, went far beyond my powers to describe in words. . . ."

Everything was there in a glance at the pictures—the setting, the tackle, the clothes we wore, the boat and motor, even the twisted smile on the face of Pete Silver, our guide, as he lifted a three-pound trout from the water. Readers of outdoors magazines love to pore over details like these; photographs supply them as nothing else can.

I didn't, however, take those particular pictures. My friend Maury Delman packed a camera and tripod up four miles of blazed trail and stood waist-deep in Lincoln Pond while Pete and I performed within range of his telescopic lens.

Maury is a professional writer-photographer who fishes in such faraway places as Iceland and Argentina and sells his stories to the outdoors magazines. He learned the importance of pictures early in his writing career, when editors answered his story suggestions with: "The idea sounds good, but what have you got for photographs?" Today, Maury would leave his tackle box behind before he'd take off on an assignment without his camera.

The editors of travel and adventure magazines feel much the same way about illustrations for non-fiction pieces. "Photographs by the author" has been a familiar credit line on *National Geographic* articles ever since Gilbert Grosvenor started roaming the world with notebook and camera many years ago. In a recent issue of *True* magazine, eight of nine features are illustrated with photographs, two of them by the authors. A recent *Argosy* had five photo-illustrated features, two combining photography and art, and two that used art only. It's worth noting that the last two were based on fantasy and humor, subjects that don't lend themselves to camera treatment.

In the craft magazine field, the picture-story is standard: either photographs or sketches are part of the author's responsibility. Maybe you can tell a reader in words *alone* how to build an outdoor patio, but you'd have a hard time convincing the editor of *Popular Science* that this is the best way to go about it. "*Top-quality photos are a must,*" he says in the magazine's requirements sheet for writers. The italics are his.

Does this mean that after mastering the techniques of writing you must start worrying about mere *pictures?* The answer is yes—if you want to sell consistently to the specialized markets. If you want, blame it on *Life, Look,* television and the man who invented the half-tone engraving process . . . but it's a picture-minded world.

Photographs won't turn a bad story into a good one but they'll often guarantee a sale that might otherwise be lost, even when the story is well written. They can also bolster a writer's income and lead to more varied and profitable assignments, once the word gets around among editors that he can deliver a complete editorial package.

Worrying about pictures has other, less tangible benefits for the writer. It helps him to observe more keenly, to look for revealing detail—colors and textures, lights and shadows, expressive forms and movements. This increased awareness of the world about him leads to sharper, more accurate reporting.

I know several writers who use the camera as a visual notebook; going over rolls of film after they come back from an assignment gives them a reliable playback of what they saw and did when they were too busy to stop and take notes.

There are four ways to get good photographs for your articles. One is to team up with a professional like my friend Maury, who is willing to share the risks and rewards of your venture. The second is to marry someone who will, patiently and expertly, take over the photographic chores while you hunt, fish or build that outdoor patio.

The third is to write only for high-budget publications that provide a staff photographer. The fourth is to learn something about photography yourself. I'll address the rest of my comments to the 90 percent or more of all working writers who are in this latter category most of the time.

Shooting your own story illustrations isn't as difficult as you might think. Editors aren't looking for prize-winning salon pictures; they expect clear, sharp photographs that put the reader on the scene and help fulfill the promise in the story title. If you have a fair amount of pictorial sense and are willing to study the fundamentals, you can probably meet the editors' requirements and have fun doing it.

Norman Phillips, a West Coast outdoors writer, looks at the matter this way: "Some writers feel that it's necessary to hire a photographer to handle the camera work. I can't see it, because with modern high-speed films and a simplified camera, anyone who can't learn to take an acceptable picture isn't smart enough to be a writer, anyway. And you still have to tell the hired photographer what shots to take and where to take them from; only *you* know what will tell your story and express your point of view. Having figured it all out, why not push the button yourself?"

Now, let's remove another mental block that sometimes gets in the writer's way. You don't need a closetful of expensive equipment to take good illustration photos, any more than you need an IBM typewriter or a gold-filled pen to write good stories.

Consider the experience of a Famous Writers School instructor who took a vacation trip to the Far East last year. With some misgivings she bought one of the new automated cameras and started shooting. She didn't see the results of her work until she got back to Westport and the processor handed her a set of pictures that would do nicely as illustrations for a travel article. Her comment was highly revealing: "You mean *I* took *those?*"

In photo-illustration, equipment is a means not an end. It's far more important that you train yourself to apply your writer's judgment to photographic problems. If that sounds like a contradiction in terms, here are a few suggestions to make the point clearer.

Good photographs, like this shot of Hong Kong harbor, are an important asset to a travel article.

1. *Plan your shots.* When a writer sits down to compose an article he uses some kind of outline, mental or written; he thinks out the story before he writes.

This planning phase is just as important when you turn photographer. Study both the picture possibilities and your story needs before you start shooting, then build a rough work plan (photographers call it a "shot list") assuring a photographic record rather than a series of random snapshots.

For example, if you're covering a deer hunt, you'll need more than a pictorial account of the hunt itself. You'll want some pictures of the base camp, close-ups of the hunters, views of the country you're hunting over, and more close-ups of the hunters bringing the deer, if any, into camp.

If you miss some key items on your shot list, or if the light isn't right, you can probably get your companions to re-enact the scene for you next day. A good many photos are taken after the event. This isn't fakery, as long as the pictures are a fair approximation of what actually took place.

2. *Put variety into your pictures.* You know how dull a piece of writing becomes when sentences and paragraphs all begin and end the same way. Sameness can be deadly in photographs, too. So vary your shooting distances, camera angles and lighting effects.

Mix long shots (25 feet or more away) with medium shots (10 to

12 feet) and close-ups (as close as you can get). For a change, try shooting *up* at your subject from a low angle, with the sky as a plain, contrasting background. Then find a rise of ground and shoot *down* on the campsite, the hunters taking off into the woods, the boat pulling into the pier.

And remember that, whatever the camera instruction book said, you don't have to take pictures with the sun at your back. Often, you'll get richer detail and more interesting composition with the light coming from side or front. Explore, experiment, improvise.

3. *Edit your pictures.* You edit a piece of copy when you pencil out the excess verbiage and pare your sentences down to essentials. You can edit pictures, too. In case you've never watched a picture editor at work, here's how to go about it.

When your prints come back from the processor, spread them out on a table and study them critically, just as you'd study a rough draft of a manuscript. Decide which pictures best tell the story you want to get across and discard the others, including all prints that are technical failures because of bad lighting, faulty focus or poor exposure. Remember, the editor will probably want one strong lead shot—a picture that symbolizes or sums up the story—plus a variety of medium and close shots. Choose both verticals and horizontals.

Sometimes you can save a print by cropping it so that only a portion of the pictures comes out in the enlargement. With a red or yellow grease pencil, mark off the area you want to keep and instruct the processor to make an enlargement "cropped as marked." You'll be surprised what this can do to bring up in vivid detail the important elements in your photograph.

All prints you mail out with your story should be 8x10 or larger, just as all manuscripts should be double-spaced with ample margins. Many writer-photographers find it's worth the expense to have the processing and enlarging done by a custom laboratory that will take extra pains to bring out the best in their pictures. You can probably locate a custom lab somewhere in your area.

I've saved the most important suggestion about do-it-yourself photo-illustration for the last, because I think it deserves special emphasis. It's simply this: *start in your own backyard.* Let me explain.

One of my few achievements is a certain adeptness at casting with a fly rod. I enjoy teaching others this pleasant pastime, but I always insist we practice on dry land. I'm convinced that without the distraction of fish and fisherman, anyone who isn't muscle-bound can learn to fly-cast in a few afternoons.

Camera-handling takes a little longer, but the principle is the same. Go into your backyard and shoot some pictures of your dog treeing the neighbor's cat; your daughter skipping rope; your son riding his bicycle; the birds lighting on the window-box feeder. Have the film developed and shoot some more, only this time choose new angles and a different time of day.

After you've used up several dozen rolls of film, you'll find you can handle the camera controls with ease and assurance and that you've learned a good deal about selecting and composing a story-telling picture. Then you can go out on an assignment with your writer's mind free to plot the sentence and paragraphs that give meaning and continuity to your illustrations.

Tape-record your notes

You might care to consider the use of a portable, battery-driven tape machine in preparing travel or outdoors articles—especially in conjunction with a camera.

Instead of writing up their notes, some writers prefer to transfer them onto a tape recording.

You shoot your pictures as you go along, and, instead of writing up your notes each day you simply dictate them to your tape machine. Of course you can also use the machine to record interviews, or to take down a commentary about a fast-moving event as it occurs. Each reel of tape should be labeled to show when it was made, where, and briefly, what's on it.

When you get home and you have your developed photographs in front of you, you can go over them and pick out the ones you want to use. Then you turn to your tapes and prepare your article outline to fit the pictures you've decided to use. In preparing the article itself, you have the full wordage of interviews to depend on, as well as detailed comment on rapid-fire events like a horse race.

As you have seen in this Lesson, travel articles and outdoors pieces have the advantage of dealing with personal experience. Writers who don't care for library research or interviewing, but who have the knack of vivid description, can do well in these fields.

The travel or outdoors writer is one of those lucky people who can have his cake and eat it, too. First, he enjoys the trip he takes; then he gets paid for writing about it.

Another large and growing market

Most free lances are well aware of the increasing demand for material among the general and even among some of the special magazines, but few know much about another large and expanding market for their output—the house organs. Here are a few cold statistics calculated to warm the hearts of all writers in search of new markets:

1. There are, by conservative estimates, more than 10,000 regularly published house organs in the United States.

2. Their combined circulation exceeds 200 million per issue.

3. The combined cost of producing a single issue of every house organ in this country amounts to more than $75 million. It's a billion-dollar-a-year business.

Now, what *is* a house organ? The following definition comes from the International Council of Industrial Editors:

The term . . . refers to many types of communications . . . issued periodically by private sponsors: business and industrial companies and various associations. They include magazines, newspapers, newsletters and mimeographed bulletins. In almost all cases they are free-circulation media, and in very few cases do they carry paid advertising.

They fall into three general classifications: internal, for circulation primarily or only among employees of the sponsor; external, for circulation among the sponsor's customers, prospects, dealers, salesmen, stockholders, among so-called thought leaders and other interested persons; and combinations of the two.

Most giant corporations are in the publishing business in a big way, producing many different periodicals. In Standard Oil of New Jersey's international network of affiliates, for instance, there are more than 300 magazines and newspapers. General Electric, which publishes a number of plant newspapers as well as magazines, runs a company-wide news service, modeled after the AP and UPI, with teletype bulletins and flashes from the home office.

Every major automobile manufacturer publishes a number of handsome magazines, of which *Ford Times,* with its excellent artwork and professional travel articles, is among the best known. Nearly all leading companies in the fields of pharmaceuticals, insurance, oil and chemicals produce magazines which are first rate.

Most of the big magazines regularly buy free-lance material, and often their rates of payment rival those of slick newsstand publications. They also tend to like impressive by-lines. However, hundreds of less elaborate house publications welcome free-lance material and are excellent markets for beginners.

Today, the editors are striving mightily for greater recognition and higher editorial standards; they shy away from chit-chat about babies and bowling scores, so characteristic of earlier house organs. Recently ten house organ editors in New York were asked how they felt about getting free-lance material. With varying degrees of enthusiasm, each said that he'd be happy to look at whatever was sent, *provided* the writers knew the magazines and had made a reasonably intelligent estimate of requirements.

The trend toward lively reading

Heavy policy statements and statistics-laden articles on economics have long made many house organs seem dull indeed, but you can be sure that the editor didn't plan for dullness; he had it thrust upon him by company executives, who sometimes appear as though they have to say something but would prefer that no one read it. However, there's a trend toward livelier and more professional editing among house organs these days; as a matter of fact, a number of former national magazine editors are now in the field as house organ editors. At a recent International Council of Industrial Editors' annual conference, two of the most popular speakers were Herbert R. Mayes, former editor of *McCall's,* and Edward Barrett, dean of the Columbia School of Journalism, both of whom emphasized the growth of professional standards among house organs.

By far the largest number of house organs are internal—they're employee publications. What kinds of articles do they publish? Tastes differ, of course, and so do fundamental aims, but one editor recently summed up what his magazine tried to accomplish in words that should give free-lancers a clue to the requirements of many employee publications.

House organs—and there are thousands of them—publish articles on a wide range of subjects. Whatever his specialty, a writer is almost certain to find a market for his material here.

"The themes we have to hit year after year," he said, "are: 'work safely, play safely'; 'profits are essential to the health of business'; 'new products are evidence of progress'."

Such themes are basic to the employee publication, though each magazine has its own technique and approach. One free-lancer has a long list of titles for articles he can always sell to one employee magazine or another. Here are a few: "The Need for Profits," "How Big Business Helps the Community," "Is Bigness Badness?" "The History of the Corporation," "Let's Cut Taxes." Never misses, he says. The demand from editors of employee magazines is insatiable.

For free-lancers, though, the "externals," which go to a wider audience, offer the best and most interesting opportunities. The editors of many externals feel they're in competition with *Life, Look* and *Reader's Digest*. So they strive for wide appeal, and tend to look toward free-lance writers to help them out. Among the best-known externals are IBM's *Think,* which publishes articles on subjects of general interest to business men, and usually unrelated to business machines; the *Du Pont Magazine,* a slick four-color magazine with articles about Du Pont's products; Chevrolet's *Friends*, a lively professional magazine with a circulation of more than 1.5 million.

According to Dr. Russel J. Jandoll, head of the department of journalism at St. Bonaventure University, who made a study of house organs, the average editor of an external prefers the material of each issue to be one-third about his company, one-third of indirect company interest, and the remainder general subjects, such as travel, food, fashion, world affairs, books, sports, hobbies and general science.

Don't write a publicity release

In general, though, the articles with the best chance of being accepted are those combining some aspect of a company's activities with material of general interest. Often, free-lancers make the mistake of thinking that all house organs want a direct, drum-beating approach, and their articles tend to sound like publicity releases rather than professional magazine pieces. The *Lamp* received a story about one of Standard Oil's marketing affiliates in typical news-release form:

The Carter Oil Company, an affiliate of Standard Oil (N.J.), is expanding its marketing operations in the Pacific Northwest, especially in the Columbia River Basin, where the desert is being reclaimed by irrigation from the Grand Coulee Dam. Six new service stations have been erected, and more are in the planning stages. . . .

In an effort to interest a wide audience, the *Lamp* linked Carter's expansion with the dramatic changes taking place in the area. Here's how the lead was rewritten:

Dust devils whirl like ghosts through the parched sagebrush east of the Columbia River, and rainfall, when it comes at all, is merely a soft spattering upon the unquenchable soil.

After vividly describing the desert before the irrigation project and the upsurge in growth after the land had been reclaimed, the piece introduced the company angle in this way:

Attracted by the exciting promise of the irrigation project, people from all over the country are coming to eastern Washington. New companies are moving in, too. Among them is the Carter Oil Company, a Jersey affiliate.

With all the talk about "public images" and such, business now makes an effort to be less stuffy and self-conscious. Even insurance companies have turned away from traditional solemnity. Time was when they used words of this sort:

It behooves every policyholder to become well-acquainted with the terms of his contract . . . .

In its lively magazine *Minutes,* however, the Nationwide Insurance Company takes a more lighthearted view:

They're not exactly what the book publishers call "hammock literature," but—believe it or not—your insurance policies can give you hours of profitable reading.

The trend reflected in many house organs today is toward an easy, natural style—a more human approach to the business of business.

For writers who have a knack of describing technical or scientific developments, there's a great opportunity among the house organs. Industrial research laboratories are forever coming up with new developments and new products. The important thing to remember about such technical pieces is that most readers are more interested in what the product or development will do for them than in the whys and wherefores of it. In other words, it's almost always best not to be too technical.

Of course, you have to be technical enough to be convincing. But when you overload your material with scientific data, when you weigh down your text with jargon familiar only to specialists in the field, you're in trouble. A reader isn't likely to spend much time with your piece if he doesn't understand it. And the same is true of editors.

Amateurs are more likely to fall into the trap of getting over-technical than professionals. By way of example, here's how a newcomer to popular technical writing might go astray in an article about research into turbine-powered automobiles:

Scientists in white smocks are scurrying around Detroit's automobile research laboratories looking for a way to adapt the gas turbine wheel that will withstand 2000° Fahrenheit in the compressor where heat and energy provide the power to turn a second turbine, which in turn turns the rear wheels.

Here's a more appropriate lead for the same story:

In the research laboratories of Detroit's car manufacturers an eerie, whistling sound, as of cyclonic winds rushing through a tunnel, issues from behind doors closed to all but the engineers and technicians who work there. This strange sound may be heralding the start of a new era in the history of the automobile.

A turbine-powered car flashes past the grandstand during the running of the Indianapolis "500" auto race.

Personality stories are always a good bet, and an almost sure sale if the man you portray has some direct connection with the company. Most editors, for instance, favor stories about employees who participate in community affairs and local politics, or who have achieved some distinction with unusual hobbies.

Company magazines these days are also trying to treat executives in somewhat less stilted and formalistic terms than they used to. The old way was to be coldly objective and remote:

Mr. Frank Thompson, after 45 years' service with American Co-Ordinates, Inc., has retired as executive vice president, a position which he assumed in 19—, after having served as Plant Manager in the Newark Co-Ordinates Works since 19—. He was president of the Co-Ordinates Association in 19—, and associate director of the Blue Feather Drive in 19—. He was a well-known and capable spokesman for free enterprise.

Editors nowadays try for a less wooden approach:

It's characteristic of Frank Thompson that, in his farewell talk to his associates at a party in his honor, he should mention the novel *Candy,* Homer's *Iliad,* the statistics of sewage disposal in Laredo, Texas, and the "Song of Solomon" to make a point about the future of American Co-Ordinates, Inc. He brought a wide-ranging and active mind to his post of executive vice president. He was also a great, free-wheeling story teller, and an unbeatable poker player.

Of course, house organs vary widely, as companies do, and it's extremely difficult to generalize about them. Every house organ editor faces the specter of the executives above him, and usually it's their judgment and taste that prevail. House organs shy away from controversy. Editors are eager to cram articles full of color and anecdote, but it's always well for a free-lancer to keep in mind that the house organ is part—probably a very expensive part—of the company's public relations program; it has nothing to do with "fearless journalism."

Such restrictions are a minor part of writing for house magazines, and all writers encounter similar frustrations. The important point to remember is that the whole house organ field does offer a large and challenging area for free-lance writers, and many beginners will surely first see their work in print there. They offer a wide variety of subject matter and approach from the very simple to the highly sophisticated. It's mainly a matter of looking around and seeing where you might fit in.

One great advantage is that the house organ market isn't concentrated in the East, as is most general publishing. The chances are good that there are several house organs published within visiting distance of your home, and these are probably the best to focus on, at least at first. The advantage of being able to talk over your story ideas with an editor can scarcely be overestimated. Also, if you live close by, the editor welcomes the fact that you're available for last-minute revisions. Soon, he may feel that he can call upon you for help during the inevitable crises that arise.

Several free-lancers have approached the house organ field from another angle. They've looked around their town or city and sought out companies who didn't have house organs, and then offered to edit one on a free-lance, part-time basis. It's safe to assume that any company with 100 or more employees has some kind of a "communications problem" which a regularly published paper or magazine would help to alleviate.

If such a suggestion doesn't ring the bell, you might follow it with another: Let the company buy a page or two in the local newspaper at regular intervals for company news and policy statements. This is done frequently, and would provide you with an interesting spare-time job, one that would help prepare you for any kind of writing you plan to do.

Such editorial work sometimes leads a free-lancer into other and more lucrative assignments for the company. There's much demand for editorial help in modern business: the manual for new employees, product brochures, executive speeches, annual reports. In a relatively short time, you may find yourself a pro in a field that is certainly growing in importance and stature.

The market for travel articles

Twenty-five years ago, it wouldn't have been worthwhile including the travel category in this Lesson. But today, thanks to more money, more leisure, the automobile and the jet plane, millions of people who used to be content to read about travel or confined their jaunts to areas near home, now go to faraway places. Hence, information about where to go, and what to do when you get there, finds an eager reading public. Here's what a free-lance travel writer had to say after he'd flown back from

Europe: "I'm a jet-age travel writer—an instant Magellan. Last week Paris. Today Mexico City. Next week, who knows?"

He said that for the past year or so he'd written nothing but travel pieces, and was doing very well because of the demand for them from the magazines. "The whole country's on the great Go Now—Pay Later kick," he said, "Swoosh, you're in Madrid! Swoosh-swoosh, you're in Hawaii! And swoosh-swoosh-*swoosh*, you're in Bangkok! So naturally travel articles are in demand. People want to know where to go, what to see. And they want to read all about it again when they get back."

Today, travel writing has a prominent niche in literature and journalism, and there's no question the niche is getting bigger. Most established magazines, even the women's service magazines, have increased space devoted to travel articles, and so have the newspapers. Guidebooks of all kinds—Poor Man's, Rich Man's, Gourmet's, Wine Drinker's, to mention only four out of many—come off the presses in a flood.

After more than 75 years of stately growth, the *National Geographic* calmly but firmly pushed above 5,500,000 circulation for the first time. And *Holiday* magazine has achieved a reputation for quality, wit and maturity far beyond its years. This vast and growing market is supplied by writers of many different tastes and talents. It would almost seem there is room somewhere for any writer who studies the market and who knows the editorial preferences of the publications he's aiming for.

Literary standards and policies vary widely, and what's just wrong for one may be just right for another. To catch a glimpse of such variance in editorial taste, let's look at the openings of two stories in *Holiday* and the *Geographic*.

First consider the lead paragraphs of Part II of "A Stranger in New York" by V. S. Pritchett, prominent British novelist, short-story writer and critic. Judging from the frequency of his appearance in its pages, Pritchett is a *Holiday* favorite.

There is a strong case to be made against New York, and particularly against Manhattan. In many respects it is the case against all great modern cities and the life they offer. Architects like Le Corbusier and Frank Lloyd Wright have attacked Manhattan's buildings and its lack of design; for with the exception of Central Park, little has been planned as a whole. Hardly a building is situated—the Seagram being one of the few "placed" buildings in the city, along with those of Rockefeller Center.

The skyscrapers were described by Gorki in 1909 as a jaw load of rotting teeth and mere stumps. The world has, however, gradually come to admire them through a trick of the eye; we rarely see them individually but only as an aggregation. But the inhabitant knows that the more the city soars the worse the stink and confusion at the foot. Architects have turned into engineers, bewitched by function.

The world-famous Australian marine author, Alan Villiers, has written many articles about his seafaring adventures for the *National Geographic.* Here's how he began a piece titled "Fabled Mount of St. Michael":

Suddenly the sea mist lifted in just one place over the land to the north of us. A ray of sunlight broke through, like a floodlight. Silhouetted against the gray was the most fantastic castle I had ever seen, a fairytale place of shining white upon a perfect plinth of its pyramidal hill.
Spired and turreted, the fortress rose with such symmetry and grace that it was difficult to see where man's work began and nature's ended. For the castle blended into the hill, and the hill carried the castle as if it had grown there, right out of the tumbling sea.
"St. Michael's Mount!" shouted the seaman beside me.

Though the two pieces differ widely in subject matter, the style and tone of each represents the magazine in which it appears. Pritchett's piece is amazingly critical by any standards of travel writing. Villiers by contrast, is boyishly enthusiastic. Pritchett's style is sophisticated, personal, subjective. Villiers concentrates completely on evoking a vivid picture of the scene before him.

Other well-established magazines in the field have different approaches. There's *Travel,* for instance, a magazine published for more than 65 years and directed not so much at the armchair adventurer as to the person about to take off on a trip. It's full of specific tips about things to do and places to go.

The lead paragraph of an article by Dick Momsen, Jr., called "Portugal's Mondogo Valley," is a fair example of its feature-article style:

Probably the most picturesque, varied and yet most overlooked region in Portugal is the valley of the Mondogo River. Starting high in the Serra da Estrela, whose 5,000-foot crest supports the country's only organized ski resort, the river winds through a narrow gorge until a 180° bend takes it out among the jumbled hills that reach nearly to the Atlantic. These widen out below Coimbra to accommodate a broad flood plain, presided over by a brooding Moorish castle. At the fishing village of Figueira da Foz, the Mondogo empties into a sea over a shallow bar marked by long rolling breakers.

This is good, colorful reporting, but the author's own feelings and impressions scarcely intrude upon the scene.

Arizona Highways, a magazine published monthly by the Arizona Highway Department but widely known for its pictorial and editorial excellence, manages to strike a note of general interest while confining its subject matter to Arizona. Typical of its direct and simple style is this lead by Rosalie Goldman in an article, "The Wrinkled Pink Walls of Kanab Canyon":

Arizona has a lost canyon. If not lost, it is overlooked. Yet it is a major canyon, over one hundred miles long. It is Kanab. Only a handful of people has been in it since a Powell survey quit the Colorado River at Kanab canyon in 1872. The gold rush may have brought a few prospectors in it before that. U.S. survey maps on the larger scale are not even available for its lower end. Kanab fills its many roles unknown, unspoiled, unvisited.

Simplicity is certainly the keynote here, but there's also a kind of poetic feeling in the final lines.

Many of the flourishing men's magazines publish travel articles, often in connection with an international sporting event or with a strong topical angle. "Canoe Racing's Drop Dead Derby" by Robert Warner in *Saga* begins in a terse, reportorial style fairly typical of that magazine's tone:

On September 5 on an inside page of a small town weekly newspaper, the *St. Maurice Valley Chronicle* of Three Rivers, Quebec, there appeared a short account of the toughest and most important canoe race on earth—the annual 125-mile sprint down the St. Maurice River from La Tuque to Three Rivers. Even though Three Rivers is less than 100 miles from Montreal, that big city's two leading newspapers, the *Gazette* and the *Star,* ignored the race completely. There was no radio coverage outside of a small local Three Rivers station and no prerace advertising.

Despite the lack of publicity, the Three Rivers police estimated that a crowd of 100,000 spectators turned out, while the Provincial police pegged the attendance at 125,000. Both explained that the 1963 turnout was much smaller than usual because of very bad weather the first day. In 1962 the crowd exceeded 150,000.

This striking photograph helped illustrate an *Arizona Highways* article on Kanab Canyon—a lost canyon which only a few people have visited since its discovery nearly 100 years ago.

As exemplified here, *Saga* likes the drama of little-known events as a peg on which to hang a story. The writing is brisk, forthright, not much concerned with local color or stylistic niceties. It's a good idea for the aspiring travel writer to make such comparisons of the magazines he hopes to write for, because each is sure to have certain quirks of policy and taste that a little study will reveal.

Except in the straight "Baedeker" kind of article, which simply reports the principal places of interest, hotels, restaurants and so on, a writer must try to capture the spirit and feeling of a place in order to make the reader know what it's like to be there. There are countless ways of doing this, but beginners often make the mistake of thinking that description alone is enough. It almost never is, simply because description is usually static. Telling the story in narrative form helps, because the reader then anticipates what will happen next.

Traveling is fun, and so, usually, is writing about it. There's something less restricted, less formal about travel stories than about other kinds of non-fiction. It also can be more of a personal expression, for the travel article admits to almost any kind of writing, as long as it's effective. *Holiday's* essays are the reflections of strong personalities and intelligent, inquiring minds who bring wit and perception and grace of style to their articles. *Holiday* has, in fact, considerably raised the standards of travel writing by insisting on high literary quality.

The excellence of travel writing lies more in the writer than in the things he perceives. All good travel writing nowadays has a personal quality, a kind of poetry and analysis, that lifts it above the simple reporting of facts.

It would probably be more helpful for the beginning travel writer of today to read contemporary books of travel, such as Alan Morehead's *The White Nile* and *The Blue Nile*, Leigh Fermor's *The Traveler's Tree*, Lawrence Durrell's *Bitter Lemons*, to name just a few, than to struggle through the "classics" of travel literature. This advice isn't intended to deprecate the classics; they simply aim at a different target.

Until the jet age, travel writers often addressed an audience they knew would never see what they were describing. They emphasized the marvels they came upon. Some of them—Marco Polo, Richard Burton, Charles Doughty and Lafcadio Hearn—

were even great reporters. Today's highly skilled travel writer
knows well that he's talking about things his audience may see
for themselves. So his aim is to interpret, to make his audience
feel as he does, to share his experiences and his insights. Instead of wonder, we now get analysis.

Nevertheless there's a classic model for the travel writer of
today—a little book by Robert Louis Stevenson called *Travels
with a Donkey*. Stevenson here captures, in style and viewpoint,
just what the modern travel writer strives for: a simple narrative style that evokes by the unerring choice of detail the essence of the travel experience. Here's how he describes waking
in a sleeping bag in a pine forest in southern France:

Frontispiece drawing
from Robert Louis
Stevenson's *Travels
with a Donkey*.

When that hour came to me among the pines, I wakened thirsty. My tin was standing by me half full of water. I emptied it at a draught; and feeling broad awake after this internal cold aspersion, sat upright to make a cigarette. The stars were clear, coloured, and jewel-like, but not frosty. A faint silvery vapour stood for the Milky Way. All around me the black fir-points stood upright and stock-still. By the whiteness of the pack-saddle, I could see Modestine walking round at the length of her tether; I could hear her steadily munching at the sward; but there was not another sound, save the indescribable quiet talk of the runnel over the stones. I lay lazily smoking and studying the colour of the sky, as we call the void of space, from where it showed a reddish gray behind the pines to where it showed a glossy blue-black between the stars. As if to be more like a pedlar, I wear a silver ring. This I could see faintly shining as I raised or lowered the cigarette; at each whiff the inside of my hand was illuminated, and became for a second the highest light on the landscape.

Of course, in the broad spectrum of travel, there's a definite place for the purely factual report. Often the lead of such a piece has some news value. The announcement of the fiesta in Trinidad, for example, would be followed by a rundown on the places a visitor should see, a list of hotels and restaurants, possibly with prices. Such stories are the bread and butter of travel writing, and many newspapers—magazines, too—often welcome articles of this kind, if they are newsworthy.

Personal travel experiences that aren't especially startling but contain information about trips others might take are also good material for stories. *The New York Times,* which now has one and sometimes two complete travel sections in its Sunday edition, often runs such stories. It's a good idea to look around your own hometown for material. After all, it might be a tourist spot for someone who lives 50 or more miles away.

With imagination, you may well find travel stories in your own backyard—or close to it. You might even make enough money from them to go to Europe or the Orient next year.

Anticipate what magazines want

Editors often get desperate for article ideas that can be tied in with holidays; *i.e.*, Mother's Day, Father's Day, Independence Day. Line up the holidays at least six months in advance and see if you can come up with some fresh ideas.

Keep the ideas or suggestions flowing. Try not to let a week go by without sending out a few ideas. Even if you are working on assignments, continue making suggestions, maintaining your vital contact with editorial staffs.

Remember, too, you can never know for sure what will strike an editor's fancy. Over and again, I've sent out ideas which I felt had practically no chance of being accepted, yet an editor said "yes." While you have to know your markets and keep abreast of what editors are looking for, it never hurts to let your imagination soar a bit and hit them with odd-ball ideas.—Robert Gaines in *A Treasury of Tips for Writers*

What about length?

Newspapers: The unit of length is the column. A story can be one column, two columns, a quarter-column and so on. In round numbers, a column is 1,000 words or four pages of typescript, double-spaced.

Magazines: Shorts, fillers and features—or more correctly, feature articles. Shorts are brief, odd items, 100 words or less and complete in themselves. Magazines (and newspapers, too) use them to fill a column, or the bottom of a page if the story or article doesn't fill the allotted space exactly.

Fillers are brief articles, usually under 500 words, and again are used to fill space.

Features, or full-length articles, can run as long as 5,000 words, but the usual length is 2,500 and many articles run 1,500 or even 1,000.

The "book-length" article that some magazines use may run up to 30,000 words, though 15,000 to 20,000 is more common. Often these are condensations of full-length books.

Books: A book may be as little as 50,000 words, though some may run over 100,000 words.

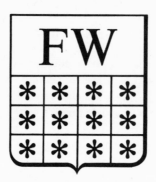

Section X

Lesson sixteen

Trade and technical articles

A trade article is devoted to the interests of a businessman in some specific trade or enterprise. A technical article, as we use the term, means a piece—at the popular reading level—about the practical, industrial or mechanical arts or the applied sciences. Pieces on hormones, home buying, new power tools, car care, miracle fabrics, convenience foods, investing, are all technical articles since they deal with a popular handling of a complicated subject.

A trade article appears in a magazine devoted to the interests of a single trade, such as these typical publications: *Boot and Shoe Recorder, Retail Grocer, Hardware Age, Dry Cleaning World, Housewares Review, Super Service Station, Candy Industry and Confectioners Journal, American Druggist* and *The Retail Digest.* Each trade magazine is devoted not only to a single trade but often to a single facet of each trade, with retail selling being the largest.

The average hardware store owner reads *Hardware Age* for only one reason—to make more money out of his store. The magazine is devoted to articles about every phase of the retail hardware business, from hiring help through stock control and actual selling to window dressing and collecting delinquent accounts. This same hardware retailer doesn't read *Retail Grocer* because the two trades are different: they have different problems and different ways of solving them.

A retailer will stick closely to his special field, even though he knows it thoroughly. So, before beginning to write for any of these specialized fields, you should study several issues of the magazines involved to make sure you know enough about the subject to interest the audience. You can't evaluate the problems of a retail clothing merchant if you don't know a good deal about the business of running a clothing store.

Examples of trade magazine writing

Let's get down to cases and look at some trade magazine articles to see what they do and how they do it. The first article is from *Cooking for Profit*. The piece is titled: "On Top of a Trend: the Pancake Inn," with the subtitle, "After Only a Few Months' Business, Management of the New 4,000-square-foot Pancake Inn in Brooklyn, New York, Estimates an Annual Gross of $450,000, some $200,000 Beyond Expectations." There is also a second subtitle, "Smart Merchandising Has Its Reward." Here is the text of the article, with our comments in the margins:

Note the "interesting statements" made in this opening: (1) Four young men; (2) An investment of $26,000; (3) Food cost of only 29 percent against average 35-40 percent.

For four young men—ages 28 to 31—who invested $26,000 to open the Pancake Inn just last October, this batter bonanza is a bit sudden. Almost before Sidney Bernstein, Al Bernstein, Stanley Yalowitz and Ed Friedman learned the true meaning of "controlled costs," they found themselves coasting along at a 29 percent level. Compared to estimates of the national average that range between 35 and 40 percent, this abnormally low "food cost" puts "P.I." management in an enviable circle.

The writer asks a question and implies that the answer is to be found in the body of the article. Note: *Nosh* is a Yiddish word meaning "more than an ordinary snack"—something rich and tasty.

Why such instant success, in the face of a softening market for pancakes? Take a look at the P.I. menu: some 100 items, from hot dogs to lobster tails. Or as Al Bernstein puts it, "From a *nosh* to a banquet. The whole family comes in. The adults order full dinners and the kids ask for pancakes. Everybody's happy." The result: a full 40 percent of the P.I.'s business is in highly profitable pancakes.

A fine, descriptive phrase: "white-napkin dinners."

Al states boldly, "I would love to sell—all day long—just pancakes, that's all." But Al is quick to admit that while the pancake image attracts curious adults and does keep the kids intrigued, much of the P.I.'s over-21 repeat-business is in first-class, white-napkin dinners. Come late evenings and weekends, though, and the P.I.'s single six-foot pancake griddle cannot keep up with the hue-and-cry for flap-jacks. On order: another five-foot griddle to be pressed into action during peak *"nosh"* periods. Co-owner Bernstein believes in travel-ing first class. "Sure," he says, "it takes a little more gas to run separate griddles for pancakes and all the other regular menu items. But it pays off . . . in pancakes that taste like pancakes."

"It takes a little more gas to run separate griddles for pancakes . . . but it pays off. . ."

Bernstein's "first-class" philosophy carries throughout his kitchen operation and out to the patron's table. Even the selection of five pancake syrups that circle the Lazy Susan on each table is, in Bern-stein's words, "the best that money can buy." He pays "10 to 12 percent" more for these premium-quality fruited syrups because he knows that he's getting "richer, better flavor." He should. Bernstein uses his own personal hydrometer to check the "Baume" or sugar count on all incoming syrups.

When the syrup salesman suggested that the P. I. trade-trial a new

Over and over again, one of the partners harps on "high quality."

The writer assumes that his educated readers know what a hydrometer is, and how to use it.

line of premium pancake syrups under consideration by the company he represented, he got a hearty "yes." Says Bernstein, "We knew he was taking a shot—just like we were. We thought we'd give him a chance." That chance came when the four partners tested syrups, pancakes and choice-of-menu in what Bernstein describes as a "family run-off." Invited to preview the P.I.'s new fare was a special group of relatives and friends of the management. The next day some 400 patrons crowded the P.I. for free pancakes and other souvenirs at the restaurant's grand opening. The unanimous verdict: the young partners had a profitable winner.

From the moment of the restaurant's grand opening, the P.I. was cooking with gas—literally and figuratively. Any lucky breaks that have come the partners' way are those triggered by hard work and punctilious planning. There's little margin for error in a restaurant that pays 52 employees some $2,600 per week to cook and serve food 24 hours a day. Bernstein knows what he wants—and gets it.

The average serving of pancakes costs just a shade over 11 cents, including syrup and whipped tub butter. ("It melts faster," says Bernstein.) Breakdown is as follows: pancakes ($0.060); two-ounce serving of syrup ($0.025-0.027); butter ($0.025). Here, Bernstein exercises three controls. The butter serving is portioned in the kitchen, as are the pancakes, using a special gun that automatically and precisely deals anything from a "silver dollar" to a gigantic "German apple."

The secret with the syrups, according to Bernstein, is to keep them just the right consistency for pouring and also make sure that the very best flavors attainable are served. In this way, the patron will not over-pour a too-freely-flowing syrup or tend to load-up on the syrup because of weak flavor.

Bernstein also folds an extra share of profits into many of his pancake specialties. His syrup supplier also happens to be a purveyor of sundae toppings. Upshot: he and the salesman concocted some fast-moving tongue tempters. Among the special pancake dishes: fold-ins of brandied peaches and fruit salad mix. In addition Bernstein uses premium-grade blueberry sundae topping in his blueberry pancake mixes and for a special "roll-up" dish.

Each table's Lazy Susan contains five sections. In special dispenser bottles that Bernstein had made: maple, blueberry, boysenberry, strawberry and honey syrups. Use-percentages: 50 percent maple; 45 percent fruit syrups; five percent honey.

Additional cost savings are realized through the use of a special batter mixing unit which can produce 100 pounds of batter in something under 17 seconds, using standard mix and ice water. Says Bernstein, "We can afford to operate pretty much on a hand-to-mouth basis so far as batter is concerned. If a weekend-run depletes our supply, we can send a man down to the cutter . . . and he's back

---

This is like the "sneak preview" of a new movie—testing audience reaction ahead of time. The reader will appreciate this.

These favorable mentions of gas as a cooking medium are prompted by the fact that the magazine is largely backed by the gas industry.

In a volume operation like this, costs are figured to a 10th of a cent. Which leads into precision again in the size of the pancakes.

The writer brightens up his copy by using the terms of the trade—"fold in." The term isn't explained, since the readers will know what it means.

Even the relative popularity of the syrups will interest the professional who wants to learn as much as he can from reading the article.

Here again "cutter" need not be explained because the readers know the terms of the trade.

in less than a minute with 100 pounds of mixed batter. Most important, our pancake batter is always same-day or even up-to-the-minute fresh."

The Pancake Inn was strictly a do-it-yourself project from the ground up. The Bernsteins, Yalowitz and Friedman were their own designer/architect team all rolled into one. The Inn's decor best could be described as contemporary, with a touch of Colonial for conversation-making counterpoint.

A total of some $100 is spent monthly on advertising by P.I. management. Most of this sum goes for take-away favors for children: wooden gliders, sheriff badges, tiny trolls or "good luck" dolls (at one cent) and balloons. The kids favorite: good old-fashioned balloons. The most expensive give-away to date is a color postcard bearing a picture of the restaurant and descriptive copy on the reverse side. But Bernstein feels that the nine-cents-per-card expenditure is more than worth it for the word-of-mouth value returned. The P.I. also makes modest space expenditures in area media.

This means just point-of-sale advertising. A restaurant with an annual gross of close to half a million dollars spends more than $1,200 a year on advertising.

The sudden success of the Pancake Inn is no big surprise to Bernstein. In the food business for some 13 years with jobs ranging from bellhop to catering-hall manager, he had been planning some sort of a pancake operation for two years prior to the Inn's official opening in October. Says Bernstein: "I saw the jammed pancake houses elsewhere throughout the New York area. So I said to myself: Why not in Brooklyn? The important thing was to have a gimmick. Our formula is simple: luxurious decor, top quality food and a complete menu—plus pancakes."

The early part of the article implied that this successful operation was the result of pure serendipity; but we see here that it was the result of two years of planning by an expert. This is useful information for the reader.

Note that this article from *Cooking for Profit* could have been written after one interview with Al Bernstein, plus a good look at the restaurant and at some of their recipes. Every word in the article is directly related to the subject, and while the piece is fully written, there are no wasted words, no padding. The writer knows what he's talking about when describing the experiences of one group of experts for the benefit of other experts in the business of selling food to the public.

The subject of this article is merchandising—how a particular business is run for profit, and by implication how restaurant people might use the same methods in their own operation. However, as far as the embryo trade article writer is concerned, this piece could be handled by anybody who:

1. Can write plain English.
2. Knows his subject.
3. Has studied his market (the magazine).
4. Has learned how to handle interviews.

Another article about merchandising

Let's examine another article stressing merchandising, this time in the stationery and greeting card field. The piece, "In-Store Convenience Attracts Drop-Ins," is from *Geyer's Dealer Topics,* a magazine aimed at office equipment and stationery dealers.

Statement of a familiar problem faced by all merchants: holding onto old customers while getting new ones. Then the promise: to tell what one merchant is doing about it.

The steps are explained one by one: go after the drop-in trade. Step two: pick the best location. Step three: get customers into the store. Step four: make shopping as easy as possible. Step five: offer a large selection of what buyers want.

Keeping your established trade and cultivating new customers is the best way to assure a thriving papetries business. The Otto Ulbrich Company, Inc., of Buffalo, New York, subscribes to this policy, and in an effort to attract an even larger clientele, the firm has moved its location to the exact center of the heaviest retail area in Buffalo.

"We set our sights on capturing as much of the drop-in trade as possible," explained executive vice-president William Goeckel. And once we had a location, which was accessible to a maximum number of people, we were determined to stress 'in-store' convenience.

"As soon as the customer entered our new store half the battle was won," said Goeckel. "The other half of the battle was to make it as pleasurable and convenient as possible for our customers to shop for cards and other stationery needs."

This was accomplished in a number of interesting ways. First of all, Ulbrich's offered its customers the most complete selection of greeting cards and social stationery items in the area and thoroughly experienced personnel to assist customers in their selection.

The greeting card department at Ulbrich's before the start of a typical business day.

"Over 200 feet of greeting card racks offer a selection that is unsurpassed in Buffalo," boasts Goeckel.

But having this vast selection also posed a problem. Some people preferred traditional cards while others tended towards contemporary cards. Mr. Goeckel had to lay out this vast display so that customers would not get confused and frustrated among the myriad of greeting cards.

An unusual but important point is made here: make sure the buyer doesn't get "lost."

To a large extent, the display problem was solved with manufacturer cooperation. Gibson Cards provided Ulbrich's with attractive electrically lighted fixtures which denoted various card categories and styles. "Our customers can easily find the classification of cards they are looking for," remarked Goeckel.

The card department a few hours later. Simple photos like these point up the success of the marketing methods discussed in the text.

Plugging the fact that Ulbrich's has the largest selection of cards and social stationery products in the area is a never-ending process. Goeckel stresses a magic word when it comes to attracting new customers: Advertising.

"About ten years ago we began to promote our greeting card department through the medium of radio," related Goeckel. "A local show called *Car & Kitchen* was chosen because of the diversified audience it attracted: housewives, commuters, etc." The Buffalo firm was able to work out an agreement with the station that soon worked to the firm's advantage.

Methods of advertising always interest the informed reader who identifies with the problems of his fellow readers.

Part of *Car & Kitchen's* format was a tri-weekly section devoted to book reviews. Since Ulbrich's has a paperback department staffed by some fairly literate individuals it was no problem for Ulbrich's to supply the station with current reviews for the broadcast purposes. In return, the station allowed Ulbrich's to use the following spot as a tie-in for blurbs about its greeting card department. Of course, the pitch changes regularly, accenting upcoming holidays and other card-giving occasions.

"We have also used radio for advertising our imprinting service," added Mr. Goeckel, "but the caliber of the personnel in this department has been the most important factor in its success. Personalized imprinting is a profitable field," he said, "but it is also very specialized and requires a lot of knowledge on the part of the sales help." Ulbrich's has two full-time clerks servicing this department. They have been with the company for 25 and 40 years respectively.

"The people in our imprinting department are familiar with printing processes, type styles and paper varieties," said Goeckel. "This accumulated knowledge allows our people to give speedy efficient service to our customers, keeping to a minimum the need to search through weighty catalogs and to guess at type faces."

Indeed, the personnel loyalty factor has been critical in the firm's success. Mr. Goeckel attributes his firm's low personnel turnover to two factors: A liberal personnel policy and a practice of hiring mature individuals. The latter policy has been highly effective in reducing the likelihood of clerks leaving their jobs as a result of getting married. "We have found that the hiring of mature individuals has been instrumental in allowing our firm to recoup the investment in personnel training," he said.

Party goods are yet another section of Ulbrich's that has prospered due to Ulbrich's combination of canny promotion and knowledgeable personnel. Ulbrich's highlights its party-goods department in large display ads in the local paper. These ads stress "brand" name, quality items and helpful salespeople. "In our advertising, we try to get the message across that we have quality wraps and favors only—no 'supermarket' items. And if you want to hold a *successful* party get the trappings at Ulbrich's," added Goeckel.

Once again, promotion can only induce the curious to come into a store, it is up to the salespeople on the line to do the final selling job. "At Ulbrich's our sales help actually helps customers plan parties. They have a wide knowledge of the materials in stock and know how to use them."

By keeping a large stock, maintaining a steady, effective promotion policy coupled with knowledgeable sales help, Ulbrich's of Buffalo is steadily achieving its goal of keeping its old customers while cultivating new ones.

Again, notice how rigidly the trade piece you have just read

Veterans in the business give experienced help in specialized departments.

The preference for older sales clerks will interest anybody who hires help nowadays.

The implication is clear: party goods don't move unless you push them. Some of Ulbrich's advertising techniques can be used by other merchandisers.

Promotion can only get the people into the store: the salespeople have to make the pitch.

sticks to the subject: it is a 750-word article and every word counts. A writer who knows the stationery and greeting card field could prepare an article like this after an interview and some on-the-spot research.

Another type of trade article

As a contrast to the piece which requires only one interview, here is another example from *Geyer's Dealer Topics,* this one about hiring sales personnel. To get data for this article, the writer interviewed one executive in Pittsburgh, three in Washington, two in Philadelphia. He could more easily have found six people in one city, but this would have given the piece too much local flavor. A magazine like *Geyer's Dealer Topics* which is distributed over a wide area wants geographical coverage in its contents, too. The article (slightly condensed by us) is titled: "Selecting Good Outside Salesmen."

What qualities should a dealer seek in a prospective outside salesman or designer?

"Good character, primarily," says Robert Dillon, founder and president of Dillon Office Furniture Company, Inc., Pittsburgh. Dillon is convinced that embryonic sales or design talent can be nurtured and developed, but that it is very difficult—and outside the dealer's province—to remedy the character defects of an applicant. *A challenging statement like this makes an effective opening for readers of a trade magazine.*

Unlike most office furnishings and stationery dealers interviewed recently, Dillon does not consider getting and training good sales and design personnel his major problem. *Another surprising statement for the reader—it makes him want to read on.*

Because of his stress on good character, Dillon had psychological tests developed for applicants for his design and sales staff.

In hiring salesmen, he leans a little towards those applicants with a design background and tries to develop the ones selected to the stature of "professionals to the office furnishings field." He looks for a selling personality, esthetic appreciation for differences in quality and for the ability to favorably convey the "Dillon Touch." *Any businessman who hires help always wants to know how his rivals go about it, rightly or wrongly.*

In evaluating an applicant for a design post, Dillon looks for not only design ability but the competence to express design concepts, to present them and, if necessary, to defend his design ideas.

Dillon is proud of his organization's philosophy, "The Dillon Touch," which he defines as "availability to the customer's needs."

Dillon points out that since founding his company he has tried to develop his staff to the point where each member can serve the total needs of every customer.

Samson B. Stern, of Stern Office Furniture, Washington, also

If good photos aren't available, put your ingenuity to work.
A montage of newspaper help-wanted ads, for example, could serve to
illustrate a trade article on finding and hiring outside salesmen.

Stern sees the sales help problem as a tremendous one; Dillon doesn't see it as a major issue. Contrasting views like these make for a good article.

stresses that the applicant must be morally and ethically correct. In addition, he looks for the person who will relate to the established group.

Stern describes finding and training outside salesmen as a tremendous problem entailing great cost to the dealer. "And don't expect a return on your investment in three to six months," he says. "It may take up to fifteen months before the new man pays off with high quality business."

Stern looks at the prospect in a selling situation. "If the applicant can sell the interviewer, he should be able to sell the customer later.

"We prefer the person who participates in civic organizations and community affairs. And the applicant should, of course, be thinking about a long-term job; he should want to grow with our company," Stern says.

Granted the dealer knows the qualities he seeks in prospective members of his staff. How does he screen the applicants who present themselves? Some screening however informal, is involved in every choice of one applicant over others. If the selection is haphazard, however, the dealer may later find he has picked a person who is alienating customers, causing the company a financial loss and, sometimes, even victimizing his employer by outright dishonesty, as the manager of one stationery store observed.

"We never hire on the first interview," Stern says. "We let him look us over and we look him over. We do not even give him an application for employment at this time. If he's anxious for the job, he'll push for it. Especially if he is applying for a sales spot, he should be aggressive in an inoffensive manner."

The applicant at Charles G. Stott & Company, Inc., Washington, D.C., is interviewed by several men to give the company a rounded opinion. If he survives these interviews, the prospect is then interviewed by the company president. The candidate must also pass a three-hour sales aptitude test.

Stern's had a local psychologist devise tests for prospective staff members. Salesmen employed by the Washington dealer at the time volunteered to be interviewed by the psychologist who sought to assess the motivation, intelligence and other success ingredients of the most successful staff members. Tests were then constructed which would disclose whether a prospect possessed these qualities.

"Of course, the tests are not infallible," Stern points out. "We have had applicants who showed up well in the tests but failed on the job, while some who appeared mediocre according to the tests, turned out very well."

Before hiring a person, Stern's draws a credit report on the prospect. "This will show a lot of related information such as marital status and any arrest record," Stern notes.

Both Stern's and Stott's have extensive programs for training the applicants they select. Neither company believes in sending a trainee out with a senior salesman.

"The senior salesman has his own work," Henry A. Niven, Jr., of Stott's points out. "And while he may be a good salesman, can he impart his knowledge to the trainee?"

However, the sales manager at Stott's closely supervises the new man's training. Until he acquires a good product knowledge, the trainee spends four hours inside the store daily. He is enrolled for the NSOEA study courses. As he progresses, he is given a few smaller accounts to handle, and for the first three to six months is required to turn in call reports.

The trainee at Stern's spends a minimum of four weeks working in the warehouse where he learns how the furniture is assembled. For the sales trainee, the time in the warehouse provides valuable product knowledge; for the design novice, it affords the first-hand information needed to produce schematic drawings. Occasionally, the new man will go along on deliveries so, as Stern points out, "If you

The screening of personnel is another subject of universal interest to businessmen because it is directly related to profits.

Compare the qualities that Stern looks for with those Dillon regards as important. The Stott Company, in turn, has very different ideas.

These ideas on training will interest any executive who has anything to do with the selling end. NSOEA stands for National Stationery and Office Equipment Association. But the writer doesn't have to tell the readers of this magazine; most of them are probably members.

sell a 20-foot conference table, you can see how you get it into the conference room."

The schedule of training at Stern's includes factory visits, meeting factory representatives and working under the supervision of the sales manager. Although Stern does not believe in sending the trainee out with senior salesmen, the new man does go along on occasions when one of the design staff is making a presentation. In addition, the sales trainee spends some time in the design department to learn what information the designers need. The new man also spends a week in the office to get to know the work flow there. And all the salesmen at Stern's have attended the Dale Carnegie Sales Training School.

The article continues with interviews of executives in Philadelphia.

Writers with more than one specialty

While a man who writes in the general magazine field usually sticks to one field, most writers in the trade area have at least two and often four or more specialties. One established expert, for instance, covers drugs; baking; gift and art; leather goods. There's a good reason for this: trade magazines designed for a single field have—in comparison with general magazines—a limited circulation. Therefore, their rates of pay are low.

To make a worthwhile living in this field, a writer has to turn out a great many words. To keep from running out of markets, he plows more than one field; the last two articles above could have been written by the same person, because a man who knows stationery could readily learn about office equipment.

The trade writer can't turn out just a few hundred words a day; his output may be in the thousands. Under pressure, some of the more successful ones spin out 5,000 words a day for days at a stretch—while still finding time for travel and interviewing. Not everyone can produce reams of copy on a daily basis, but those who can, and who enjoy travel and meeting people, make a good living from it.

The needs of trade magazines

There are well over 2,000 magazines in this field and every one is specialized. Each editor knows exactly what he wants—and won't take anything else. So your first step is to decide what field to write in (ceramics, furniture and fixtures, retailing and so on). Second, pick one or more trade magazines in that field, get copies of them and learn their requirements. Third, begin preparing articles.

But how do you know what the fields are and which magazine to pick? The simplest way is to ask your librarian for the *Ayer Directory of Newspapers and Periodicals,* the most complete roster of newspapers and magazines available. It contains several listings, but the one you want is "Trade, Technical and Class Publications." This breaks down by class—aviation, dry goods, food, etc. This class in turn is broken down by states. Data on each magazine includes title, circulation and a thumbnail description of contents.

The *Ayer Directory* contains complete up-to-date listings of newspapers and magazines in every major field.

While *Ayer* gives the names of all recognized trade and technical publications, it gives no details. Another source to consult is the *Annual Business Publication Guide,* published by *Industrial Marketing,* 740 North Rush Street, Chicago 60611. This *Guide* gives the name and address of a publication, how often the magazine is published, the name of the editor and, usually, circulation as well as single-page advertising rate. (This last is a rough index to the rates of payment you may expect: if the page cost is high, so, in most cases, is the compensation.) There's also a cross index of magazines by field—leather, mining, packaging, etc. In all, the *Guide* lists some 2,400 publications.

From here, your job is to get copies of the magazines, study them and begin digging for material. The writing itself is no different from other non-fiction writing, as long as you keep in mind the man you're writing for: he's a merchant who wants to run his business better. He wants no fancy writing, no involved explanations; he wants facts, simply presented. If the piece can be illustrated with photographs (or even simple diagrams), so much the better.

When you feel you know enough about a subject, start your interviews. Talk to store or business owners; explain that you want to write about new ideas they may have for (you name a leading magazine in the field). Most people are flattered at the idea of appearing in print and if you catch your man when he's not too busy, he'll talk readily.

When you have enough notes for an article, begin writing. At this point you have a choice: you can either write a full article and send it in, hoping it's close enough to the editor's requirements; or better, write up your notes and send a query to the editor. If he reacts favorably, finish your article, incorporating any ideas he may suggest. If he says "No," go to the next magazine on your list and try again.

Your letter of inquiry has two things to sell: your story and yourself. The story is the important thing. Write a résumé of it, making clear how your story fits *his* requirements. At the end, put in a few lines about yourself—who you are and what you've published. And be sure to include return postage with your letter.

If you plan more than part-time work at trade writing, there aren't enough stores and businesses in one community to keep you supplied with ideas. You'll have to travel, probably to several towns and cities. In a few months you can work out a regular route to cover. With several fields of interest, you can make stops in each town and by the time you start around your "territory" again, most of the merchants will have had time to develop something new for you.

Where do ideas come from?

The answer is—from looking and asking questions. After a writer has learned about a trade or business, and become familiar with the requirements of one or more of the magazines serving that trade, he visits stores to see what looks fresh and different. Sooner or later he'll spot an idea. Then he gets enough detailed information to make an article. He may interview one man or many, visit one store or plant, or several. What he gets may be something actually new, or more likely, a new approach to something old.

For instance, stores have had show windows for hundreds of years; men's shoes are familiar; yet a fresh way of displaying men's shoes in a store window is new, therefore interesting to *other shoe-store owners*.

An imaginative new way to display merchandise in store windows is always of interest to other store owners—and always a good prospective subject for a retail trade magazine article.

Merchandising is the area of interest to most trade readers. From your point of view, the fact that there are many ways to talk about the subject makes it a good one for you. Any business which has something to sell (and that means most businesses) has a method of selling, so a new approach to some phase of selling makes it a story prospect. It's up to you to find out the difference in the method or approach, and present it so it will interest other merchants in the same business. Whether you are dealing with a chain of supermarkets or a store on the corner, you find out what's new in moving merchandise, since that's what the trade readers want to know.

Even such things as hiring personnel or handling credit are, in the large sense, a part of merchandising, for they reflect on the efficiency of a business and hence on the balance sheet at the end of the year. To show some of the trade article possibilities, here's a nine-point breakdown of just one sector of selling:

Sales plans
To promote some specific article.
To promote a group of articles.
To promote an industry as a whole.
To promote a city and obtain new industries.
To promote some specific service.
To promote the merchants on a specific street.
To promote new charge-account customers.
To promote a trade-mark or trade name.
To promote sales management meetings.

This general list could easily be extended, but let's see how such items would be handled in a specific case:

Window displays

Purpose
1. To promote a specific article of merchandise.
2. To promote a group of related items.
3. To cooperate in a city-wide campaign (Old Home Week, Clean-Up-Paint-Up Week, etc.).
4. To promote goodwill in general.
5. To promote a service.
6. To introduce a new product.

How arranged
1. Style and treatment.
2. New materials used.
3. Cooperation of other merchants.

4. Special seasonal displays.
5. Tie-in of display with store interior.
6. Display in vacant store-building windows.

These twelve items don't by any means exhaust the material on window displays. Whole books have been written on the subject. Almost any trade journal read by retailers is open to articles on window display—not general articles but stories slanted toward their respective groups of readers.

Suppose we take one of the twelve headings above and see what information you need to write the story. For instance, *style and treatment*:

1. Name of individual in charge.
2. Years of experience (to establish authority for his remarks).
3. Why he selected this particular style and treatment.
4. Is it mass or individual display?
5. Reason for linear arrangement (verticals, horizontals, diagonals, curves, squares, etc.).
6. Color treatment.
7. General or spot lighting.
8. Does he design window in advance or build as he goes?
9. Part played by background.
10. Is there a planned relationship between merchandise and window cards?
11. Does window produce planned emotional effect?
12. What extra expense for accessories?
13. Careful description of window and merchandise displayed.
14. Public reaction in terms of sales.

With this information, you should be able to write an article enabling other merchants, if they so desire, to follow this man's suggestions. And the story should of course be illustrated with photographs. This brings us to another important point.

To photograph or not to photograph

Increasingly, the answer is "Yes" in the trade magazine field. Virtually all editors say that they want photographs, and a few have begun to say they won't take articles without them. This leaves you with three choices:

1. Get a photographer to take pictures for you.
2. Secure them, when you can, from a manufacturer.
3. Take them yourself.

Let's talk about each of these. But first, two preliminary points. What kind of pictures are you going to supply? The answer is, nothing fancy, just good, simple 8x10 photographs. If you're talking about the layout of a store, the editor wants a couple of pictures which show clearly how the store is laid out, nothing more. Second, how much are such pictures worth? Usually between $5 and $10 for each 8x10 glossy print.

Now let's go back to Point 1 above: having a professional shoot pictures for you. You'll get good pictures, but probably all the money will go to the photographer. Further, you'll have trouble in making appointments, transporting the photographer, supervising the shooting and picking up the prints. In short, you're going to a lot of bother for no additional income.

Point 2: getting pictures from a manufacturer. If, say, you're writing about a new type of light fixture, the manufacturer's public relations department will be happy to supply you with excellent pictures. But such pictures, while good, are usually not what you have in mind; they don't fit your article.

Point 3: take the pictures yourself. This is by far the best. You are in control; you shoot what you want, from the angle you like. All you need is a camera, plus a flash gun, some bulbs and a little practice. And even after paying for the processing, you can make a small profit on each photograph you sell.

New easy-to-operate photo equipment has made it possible for the amateur to take passably good photographs to illustrate his articles.

Writing technical articles

The field here is enormous, running all the way from a piece on the newest developments in house paint for magazines like *Popular Science* to an article on Bessel Functions for the *Journal of the Mathematical Society*. However, this Lesson will talk about the "popular" level of writing—articles that can be read and enjoyed without special education or training. Although we have already discussed popular science articles in Lesson Thirteen, we return to the general subject at this point because of its relationship to trade press writing.

You can find technical articles in almost every type of magazine. A magazine for antique lovers may carry a piece on the decorative motifs favored by the Adam brothers; a farmer's magazine will contain a piece on the latest findings about artificial fertilizers; a woman's magazine offers articles on the late trends in decoration, and so on. Basically, technical articles supply information about an art, profession or craft.

The first requirement of a technical article is that it furnish a typical reader with information he didn't have before. This means, of course, that the writer must know considerably more about a subject than his reader knows. Let's analyze a couple of technical articles and see what makes them work. Naturally, the articles we cite are comparatively simple, since we can't assume special knowledge on anyone's part. We'll begin with a feature from *Science News* about a subject of universal interest—food.

Man is capable of using up the resources of the ocean just as he is those of the land, and if he is going to exploit them intelligently, he has a lot to learn. A rough picture of one marine food chain shows that 10,000 pounds of microscopic plants (phytoplankton) are converted into 1,000 pounds of small drifting animal life (zooplankton). They continue the chain by becoming 100 pounds of herring, which become 10 pounds of baby tuna, which finally become a single pound of adult tuna.

We've been told so often about the sea representing an inexhaustible source of food that a startling statement like this induces us to read on.

The efficiency ratio of this process is 10,000 to one. Other than that, knowledge is sketchy, and although we know the quantities of plant life and the resulting amount of fish, there is much that needs to be filled in about the stages in between.

We may never have used the term "efficiency ratio," but we can assume what it means here.

"The old descriptive methods are insufficient for studying the biological resources of the ocean," said Soviet biologist Dr. M.E. Vinogradov of the Institute of Oceanology in Moscow.

The kind of information presently available is simply not complete

enough to guide economical utilization of the ocean, but newer mathematical research techniques are already in use in the USSR, he told the Second International Oceanographic Congress in Moscow.

The general outlook at the moment is pessimistic. The world's annual fish catch went up from 23 million to 46 million tons between 1953 and 1963 and is now estimated at 50 million tons, but scientists do not expect it to double every decade indefinitely.

This sounds like a lot of fish, but don't forget that the sea is a source of food for domestic animals as well as for people.

Most of today's principal fishing grounds are set at top capacity and future increases will have to come from exploitation of newly studied upwelling areas where nutrients are brought to the surface in vast quantities. One zone in the Peru Current, exploited less than 10 years ago, already brings in its top limit of nine million tons of anchovies, which are processed into fishmeal to feed livestock.

Dr. David Cushing of the Lowestoft Fisheries Laboratory in England described an experiment in Scotland where baby plaice (European flounder weighing eight pounds or more when grown) are being reared within a fjord walled off by a lock. Since their mortality rate in nature is 99.9 percent, it is hoped this breeding experiment will increase their survival.

Here is a writer's error. Would you use *fjord,* a Norwegian word, to describe a place in Scotland —especially as there is the Scottish word *loch* available?

Professor T.S. Rass of the Moscow Institute of Oceanology reported experiments in acclimatizing fish to new regions, such as moving tropical milkfish from waters west of Mexico to areas off Central America.

All in all, however, the future of commercial fish populations seems limited. The biologists agreed that the combination of heavy fishing with modern, highly developed technical gear and unfavorable climatic conditions can bring about the exhaustion of a species within just a few years.

The use of three experts in this short piece gives it great authority. Their testimony corroborates the statement made in the headline which appeared on this piece: "Sea Food Exhaustible."

Science News is a magazine devoted to "a weekly summary of current science." Each article is reduced to essential facts, so that the publication may cover as many fields as possible in the brief compass of 14 or so pages. While the coverage is wide, the truly "technical" is avoided. Any reader above grade-school level, with an interest in science in its broadest sense, can enjoy the contents.

Next, let's examine a technical article from a mass magazine, *Good Housekeeping*. This one, "Rotary Power Mowers," is of interest to every householder—or wife of a householder—who has a lawn to cut. If he already has a power mower, he'll read this

The schooner *Vema* puts out to sea from the Woods Hole Oceanographic Institution in Massachusetts. The three-masted vessel stays at sea 300-plus days a year, more than any other research craft.

article to see if he can pick up useful hints about operating his machine. If he doesn't have one but is thinking of buying, he'll read it to help him make up his mind about what model to buy. Meanwhile, any reader can absorb valuable information about the safe operation of power mowers.

Power mowers have become practically indispensable to the American homeowner. At present, some 24 million are in use in this country and about 4 million more are being sold every year. Of these, approximately 90 percent are the rotary type. The reason for this marked preference is easily explained.

The rotary can do jobs which the reel-type cannot, such as cut rough, high growth and trim under low bushes. It's mechanically simpler than the reel and so can be made and sold less expensively; it also requires little maintenance.

But with all these advantages, this powerfully useful tool can be powerfully dangerous—unless you understand it thoroughly and use it with care. The lightning speed and force of cutting action that make the rotary such a successful mower also make it a potential menace.

Rotary blades travel at speeds up to 4,000 revolutions per minute; they hit with a force in excess of 10,000 pounds per square inch. A hand or foot which is inadvertently placed or slips into the cutting zone will be struck by the blades many times before it can possibly be withdrawn. Thus it is easy to see why accidents with a rotary are never minor. At the very least they involve mutilation of flesh and bones, often amputation of fingers, hands or feet.

One reason why the rotary is so dangerous is that it *looks* harmless. Its spinning blades, unlike those of the actually safer reel-type, are hidden from view under a compact housing. This puts users off their guard so that they approach the rotary without proper caution. The comparative danger goes beyond mere appearances. The rotary's large diameter and directly motor-driven blades give it a far higher blade-tip speed than the small-diameter reel, whose speed is reduced by pulleys. Objects contacting reel blades from above are usually thrown forward and down. If a hard object, picked up from the grass, gets caught between blades and bedknife, it will usually jam the reel and stall the motor.

A second source of injuries, very nearly as serious as direct contact with the blades, is flying objects—stones, toys, wire, nails, pieces of blade—hurled out through the discharge chute. Such objects can and do cause deep flesh punctures and have even caused fatalities. Sad to say, some of the victims are innocent bystanders located as far as 30 feet away. And Professor L.W. Knapp, Jr., of the University of Iowa has found evidence which indicates that the high-speed, hard objects propelled through the discharge chute aren't the only perilous

---

No explanation of the difference between the two types. Anyone who knows enough about mowers to read this article should comprehend the difference.

Use of these large numbers makes the rotor blades sound dangerous—just what the writer wants. "Accidents are never minor . . ." is a good phrase to reinforce the "danger" theme.

The writer jumps back and forth from one type of mower to the other so that the reader will comprehend the differences.

Always seek out authorities to quote in any field. Their word is much more impressive than yours, no matter how right you are.

An article on the safe operation of power mowers, although technical, often will appear in mass magazines like *Good Housekeeping*.

projectiles. Objects coming in contact with the blades can ricochet off the ground and shoot off fast and forcefully in any direction.

It is conservatively estimated that 50 million people in the U.S., users and bystanders, are exposed to power mowers yearly. If the number of possible victims is so large, and the hazards are so great, you're probably wondering what's being done to protect people from themselves and from the mower.

Naturally, the power-mower industry is deeply concerned as injury statistics mount, and is making a series of efforts to solve the problem. Among the constructive steps: a seminar held in Washington, D.C., this past February by the Outdoor Power Equipment Institute. Its purpose was to give impetus to a continuing safety campaign aimed at reducing power-mower accidents through improved machine design and consumer education. Highlight of the program is a

The reader may never have heard of this group, but even so, the name gives added weight to the article.

Mentioning a seal like this is wise, for it gives the reader something positive to look for when buying a new mower.

triangular label which you will see affixed to all power mowers that meet the American Standards Association safety specifications. These specifications provide for arrangement and design of components and selection of materials which reflect the latest knowledge of safe design. Most are features which are not readily recognizable by the average homeowner or buyer. Manufacturers were quick to adopt these standards and an estimated 90 percent of the rotary mowers sold in 1966 will meet them.

Doctors, especially those attached to hospitals, are just about the best "respected authorities." The direct quote is also effective.

Participants at the conference included, besides industry representatives, experts from government and from the medical profession whose work concerns them directly with the problem. Dr. Abraham B. Bergman of the Children's Orthopedic Hospital and Medical Center at the University of Washington underscored one significant factor when he stated: "Families who would never dream of allowing their children to operate power tools in the basement blithely let them operate this fun weapon." Moving the problem from the family backyard to the national scene, he told the assembled experts that they must perhaps consider at what point a useful product of private enterprise becomes a real public health menace. Along these same lines, William V. White of the U.S. Public Health Service's Division of Accident Prevention expressed the conviction that "the patient with a puncture wound or a severe laceration of the foot from a power-mower accident is just as sick as his neighbor who is disabled by disease."

Oddly enough, the very vagueness of this paragraph makes it effective. The figures may be even worse than you imagine.

It is not known precisely how many injuries result each year directly or indirectly from rotary mowers. However, projecting from a dozen or more localized studies across the country made since 1955, the industry knows the figure is high. Efforts are being made to collect more data on the kind of injuries in relation to machine design. The increased knowledge will greatly aid the industry's active research program geared to finding ways of making rotary mowers safer.

The writer ends on a strong note. A lawn mower is like a car; it's potentially dangerous. *How* dangerous depends on the human that's operating it.

But no matter how inherently safe the industry makes the mower, the biggest hazard to safety will always be the man behind the mower —the careless, uninformed or misinformed man who treats his high-powered machine like a plaything. This is where consumer education, of which this article is a part, comes in—instructing the user about his machine and how to operate it without danger to himself or his family.

This *Good Housekeeping* piece is a useful example of the kind of article a beginning writer could produce. The real *technical* content is small, and even this is carefully explained. The average man or woman could understand and profit from this instructive prose.

Any serious hobbyist is a potential technical article writer.

Simply by learning about his hobby, by keeping up with what others are writing about it, and by increasing his own skill, he can become an "authority" who knows more than the average writer. As soon as he reaches this stage, he becomes a technical article writer in embryo, because he can turn out information pieces for amateurs and putterers.

We shall sum up this Lesson on trade and technical writing by pointing out that trade articles are aimed at and read by businessmen looking for ways to improve their businesses. Technical articles—at the higher levels—are read by people with specialized knowledge and training who are interested in the latest theories and discoveries on the outer fringes of knowledge. However, a vast number of popular technical articles appear in mass magazines. They're written for the entertainment and instruction of that universal "man in the street."

The market in both trade and technical writing is large and growing. If either is suited to your temperament and talents, you might well consider specializing in the one that appeals to you the more.

English is a flexible instrument

Writing involves a thorough familiarity with the possibilities inherent in the use of the English language. English is a marvelously flexible and delicate instrument; it can say anything you want it to say, with clarity and with persuasiveness, and with any overtones you wish—but you have to know how to use it. And I suppose one of the best ways to become familiar with it is to absorb, endlessly, the best English writing one can lay one's hands on.

Read the good writers long enough and you finally develop a feeling for their use of words. You know good writing when you see it; you listen to it with an inner ear, so to speak, and at last you instinctively know when it is good and when it is poor. The instrument will do anything on earth you want it to do if you learn how to handle it; part of the trick lies in becoming perfectly familiar with it, and the other part lies in practicing it over and over again, until what you yourself are writing begins to make harmonious noises in that inner ear.—Bruce Catton

Section XI

Lesson seventeen

Writing non-fiction books

The experience and skill gained in writing magazine articles can be of value in creating non-fiction books. However, a non-fiction book isn't merely an extended article or group of articles strung together—and although it widens the writer's scope, it also deepens the pitfalls.

Non-fiction book writing isn't for beginners, any more than is dramatic criticism or film writing. Just the same, we believe every student should have a working knowledge of book techniques, so let's start by examining some of the differences between the average article and the average book manuscript.

The most obvious difference is in length. A non-fiction piece runs from 1,500 to 5,000 words; a book runs from 60,000 to 100,000—sometimes more. Thus, a book is roughly 20 times as long as an article. But grouping 20 random articles together doesn't make a book. A book must have a central idea or theme, strong enough to hold the reader's interest for hours. You could write a highly readable article on "The Short-Weight Racket—How Housewives Are Gypped," but a book on the subject would be monotonous.

Let's look at some of the more successful non-fiction books

of recent times and define the central idea behind each. Notice, as you look over the list, that in none of these books did the writer require special training or unusual equipment; only experience and the ability to research—things which *you* should be able to bring to the writing of a book.

1. *The Naked Society* by Vance Packard. This book describes the many ways in which the individual's right to privacy is gradually being whittled away.

2. *The Guns of August* by Barbara Tuchman. A detailed account of the early days of World War I. This was a Book-of-the-Month Club choice, a Pulitzer Prize winner and the subject of a motion picture. It is entirely the product of research.

3. *Travels With Charlie* by John Steinbeck. The adventures of a writer who went touring around the United States by car. His traveling companion was an intelligent dog.

4. *Silent Spring* by Rachel Carson. A warning of the dangers to wild life, and indeed life in general, from the unrestrained use of chemicals to control weeds, insects, rodents and pests.

5. *In Cold Blood* by Truman Capote. The lives and mental processes of two murderers and, to some extent, the effect of the crime on the community in which it happened.

6. *The Last Battle* by Cornelius Ryan. The collapse of Germany and the Nazi war machine in the final days of World War II. The story has human impact because it's told in terms of individuals and their experiences.

7. *Gift from the Sea* by Anne Morrow Lindbergh. A remarkable woman offers inspiring answers to the challenges and problems facing women.

8. *Please Don't Eat the Daisies* by Jean Kerr. The day-to-day happenings in a suburban household can become fascinating reading with the added ingredient of humor.

9. *Never Call Retreat* by Bruce Catton. The last days of the Civil War are presented in a fresh and exciting way by a master of research and literary style.

10. *Profiles in Courage* by John F. Kennedy. The lives of men familiar to everyone are turned into Pulitzer Prize material in the hands of a man who later became President.

None of these ideas may seem truly remarkable yet each of the books was outstandingly successful. The very gap between description and execution shows clearly the tremendous power of the written word when skillfully handled.

Sometimes a book can have such an impact that it affects the thinking of a nation: *Silent Spring*, for example, triggered our current concern with the destruction of natural resources. The progressive spoilage of our water supply, the ruination of beauty spots and pollution of the atmosphere had been going on for years, yet no one was paying much attention. Then came Rachel Carson's book. Now pollution control is a matter of major interest at city, state and federal levels.

Rachel Carson's *Silent Spring* made the nation aware of the dangers of pollution—like the indiscriminate use of pesticides sprayed by this crop-dusting plane—which threaten our natural resources.

We don't say that you *can't* make a book out of a collection of articles. It's done all the time. Yet the pieces *must* have a common theme, like "Hollywood Royalty—the Stories of Twenty Great Movie Personalities." Here the unifying word is "Hollywood"; many readers are fascinated by the lives of flamboyant personalities in the movie capital. But if you spliced together a book about "Twenty Interesting Personalities," thereby removing the central theme, you probably wouldn't have a success.

Thus, a book must have a strong central idea—strong enough to hold up through thousands of words and hours of reading. If this theme shows up in the title—as in the example above—so much the better.

Another difference between the article and the book is research. A non-fiction book is the end result of an enormous amount of digging. If a book is twenty times as long as an article, it should have roughly twenty times as many interesting facts. A book about real things and real people must be crammed with facts. And all the facts must deal, at least indirectly, with the central theme. For example, Bruce Catton, in writing about the Civil War, must stick to the facts of the Civil War; he can't suddenly start talking about steamships on the Atlantic—unless there's a clear connection between steam power at sea and the course of war on land.

Research for a book represents a major expenditure of a writer's time. As Rudolf Flesch points out:

Research alone will take the book writer months, a period in which he perhaps could have researched and written several non-fiction articles. The quality of the research varies, too. You hit some high spots in a magazine article. You have to fill in the spaces between those peaks in a book. For a magazine article you don't have to pretend you're an expert in the whole field of your subject.

In book writing, you can't even pretend to be an expert; you *must* be one. You must know your subject so exhaustively that other experts in the field (one of whom is more than likely to review your book) won't belittle your work on publication.

Obviously, it's easier to find an idea that will stand up for 5,000 words than one which can support the weight of 60,000 to 200,000 words. Bennett Cerf says:

A book is not only a very long project in terms of time and space and effort. It must also be sold (first to the publisher, then to the reader) on its own merits. A magazine may have many reader hooks or lures. Magazines also have predictable sales, some by subscription. They have ready, periodic audiences, plus advertising revenue. Not so a book. Sales of non-fiction books are by no means predictable and neither is the writer's income, since it's based on royalties or a percentage of the publisher's income from the sale of the book.

Where a writer will receive a set fee for a magazine piece, there's no fixed sum for a non-fiction book. It's mathematically possible that a non-fiction book will sell less than 100 copies, and if the price of the book is $5 and the author's royalty 10 percent, he's made 50 cents per copy, or about $50 for a year's work.

This is an exaggeration, of course, but it serves to define the pronounced differences between depending on article writing or book writing for a living. Naturally, most professional writers do some of both. For many non-fiction writers, though, books are luxuries. A book, says Hal Borland (who has written a dozen successful volumes and hundreds of articles), takes so long to write and its sales are so unpredictable that many writers can't afford to write one. He goes on:

Book research will require at the very least several months. The writing, even if you are a fast worker, will take a minimum of two months, more likely six months or longer. At the very best, it will take six months to generate a book idea, research it, organize it and write it. More often it will take nine months to a year.

Suppose this book, then, is placed with a publisher without delay, or suppose it is sold—contracted for—before it is written. At best, it cannot be published earlier than six months after you deliver the manuscript. (I am ignoring the *quickies*, as they are called in the trade, short books turned out with a minimum of research, written at breakneck speed and rushed into print to catch a fad-interest.) If you are fortunate, the sales may reach 7,500 copies. And don't scoff at that figure; books have been on the best-seller list with total sales less than 7,500. Your royalties on such a sale—we are pricing the book at $4 to simplify the mathematics—will be less than $3,500.

Part of those royalties will have come to you as an advance. You may have got $500 when you signed the contract, another $500 when you delivered the manuscript. Six months after publication you will get more royalties if the book's sales are sufficient to more than cover the advance and the cost of your typographical revisions on the original galley and page proofs. If it sells 5,000 copies in the first six months, the total royalties will be $2,000, of which you had $1,000 in advances. You will, then, get another $1,000 at the end of these six months. After that, you will receive royalties on succeeding sales every six months. If total sales amount to only 5,000—and that is true of many books—your total royalties are $2,000.

Consider the time and energy spent, and weigh them against the returns. It is not hard to see why the writer who earns his living at the typewriter thinks twice before he starts on a book. If he is well established as a writer, he probably can write and sell six articles in the time it takes to write a book. At the base rate, $750, paid by many magazines, those six articles will bring $4,500. In terms of dollars, and granting a book sale of 7,500 copies, it would cost him about $1,000 to write a book.

What about the satisfactions?

Despite the drawbacks to book-length non-fiction, there are many satisfactions and rewards not enjoyed by the article writer. The book has a longer life than the article, and many outlive the average novel. If the factual work keeps selling for several years (which is often the case), the writer continues to receive royalties totaling more than the fees for a score of magazine articles.

A non-fiction book is usually written *after* the writer signs a contract with a publisher. This means that publication is virtually guaranteed. An article for the general magazines, unless assigned by an editor, is a gamble on the writer's part, and for every four or five articles he writes, he may sell only one or two— or maybe none at all. Furthermore, research for a non-fiction book may unearth such a wealth of material that the author can use some of it for articles even as he works on the book. He may even find himself with enough material for another book.

As an example of this, in the introduction to her recent book, *The Proud Tower,* Barbara Tuchman says that when she had finished writing *The Guns of August* she had enough research left over for another book—*The Proud Tower* was the result. In this connection, here is the story of Mrs. Tuchman and her amazing success as an historical writer, as told in the *Famous Writers Magazine*:

When the Pulitzer Committee of the Columbia School of Journalism selected *The Guns of August* as the most "distinguished book by an American" in non-fiction, Mrs. Tuchman's success in the literary field of her choice had reached its peak. But such success had not come quickly or easily; in back of it was a long record of training, experience and sacrifice. Carried forward by a deep compulsion to write, she had burnished her style through years of intensive journalism, had observed and reported in foreign lands, and had resisted the

After completing *The Guns of August,* Barbara Tuchman had enough research left over for another full-length volume on World War I.

distractions of social and community activities at home.

"Writing is often considered too casually—like flower arranging," she says. "But actually it's a highly skilled art, requiring the same devotion and attention to work demanded of the concert pianist. A person shouldn't expect to become a professional writer with his left hand. It only happens with practice—lots of practice!"

Her interest in writing and history goes back to an early age. She always loved to read, and history began to fascinate her when she was about six through the medium of the popular *Twins* series of Lucy Fitch Perkins. "I became absorbed in the fortunes of the *Dutch Twins*; of the *Twins of the American Revolution,* who daringly painted the name Modeerf (or 'freedom' spelled backward) on their rowboat; and especially of the *Belgian Twins,* who suffered under the German occupation of Brussels in 1914."

Although she's never wanted to write fiction, as a young girl she enjoyed historical novels, the works of Scott and Dumas among them. At Radcliffe she majored in history and developed an interest in international affairs. After graduation, she went into journalism, first with the Institute of Pacific Relations, later with *The Nation.*

Seven years as a journalist gave her the opportunity to live in To-
kyo at one point and to cover the Spanish Civil War at another, experiences that deepened her knowledge of world affairs and sharpened
her powers of observation. Most important of all, her work as a reporter gave her sound basic training in writing clearly, accurately and
briefly.

Her career in free-lance writing grew out of her years in journalism, and her first book, *The Lost British Policy: Britain and Spain
Since 1700*, published under her maiden name of Barbara Wertheim,
appeared in 1938. Two years later, when she and Dr. Lester R. Tuchman were married, she gave up her career to devote herself to the
responsibilities of home and motherhood. But in 1943, when her
daughter Lucy was 18 months old and the war sent her husband to
South Africa, she joined the staff of the U.S. Office of War Information in New York City.

"There I got first-rate training," she recalls. "We worked six days
a week, and I had to turn out copy every day. News work is a wonderful background for aspiring writers." The end of the war meant a return to domesticity and two more daughters, Jessica and Alma. By
the time Alma was a year old, her mother decided to resume her writing career—this time at home. But of one thing she was certain: her
family had top priority.

Caring for three children and writing meant planning her time
carefully and sticking to the plan. Mrs. Tuchman managed to do
some writing each morning, returning to her earlier interest in contemporary history. Her subject this time was the Palestine question
and the effect of British foreign policy in the Near East. But this second book, *Bible and Sword: England and Palestine from the Bronze
Age to Balfour*, did not appear until 1956; dovetailed with caring for
her growing family, the task had required six years. Her next book,
The Zimmermann Telegram, took only two years because her children were all old enough to be in school.

This third book had been suggested by her research in *Bible and
Sword*. A dramatic moment in the Palestine situation had been the
publication in November, 1917, of the Balfour Declaration by the
British Foreign Office. Digging back into Foreign Secretary Balfour's
political career to search out the causes of his Declaration, issued
during one of the darkest months of World War I, Mrs. Tuchman
came upon the explosive incident that finally brought the United
States into the war on the side of the Allies: the notorious Zimmermann telegram.

The telegram, intercepted by British Naval Intelligence in London
and decoded in its secret "Room 40," had been sent by the German
Foreign Minister to the German Ambassador in Mexico, instructing
him to offer Mexico a slice of the southwestern United States if she
would join the Central Powers and declare war on America. With

mounting excitement Mrs. Tuchman dug into records of the National Archives and the Library of Congress in Washington and produced a fascinating narrative of international intrigue.

When she had completed *The Zimmermann Telegram,* Barbara Tuchman was more convinced than ever that non-fiction can be as fascinating as fiction if it's told in narrative form. Her viewpoint on history appealed to Cecil Scott, editor-in-chief of the trade book division of Macmillan's. After reading *The Zimmermann Telegram* he got in touch with Mrs. Tuchman and asked whether she would like to write a book about the opening weeks of World War I. The result, three years later, was *The Guns of August.*

Obviously, *The Guns of August* derives its richness from rare details, from memorable episodes and quotations and from intimate human drama. Even more than *The Zimmermann Telegram,* it is "a matter of people." It is filled with human warmth, human valor, human mistakes that cost countless lives, gleaned mostly from the diaries and recollections of men and women who lived through those first weeks of World War I.

Her fifth book deals still more deeply with the human factor in history. Foretold by the opening chapter of *Guns,* which describes the funeral of Edward VII, *The Proud Tower* covers the twenty years preceding the outbreak of World War I—the last of Queen Victoria's reign and the nine of Edward VII's.

The cream of European royalty proceeds slowly down the Mall during the funeral of England's King Edward VII.

For all of her books she has found the areas of research boundless, and hence cautions the non-fiction writer not to fall into the trap of endless collecting. She limits herself to basic sources—private letters, original reports, documents in government archives—and searches for them everywhere. *Guns* took her to the New York Public Library, the New York Historical Society Library, the Hoover Library at Stanford University, the American Ordnance Association in Washington, the Imperial War Museum in London, the Bibliothèque de Documentation Internationale Contemporaine in Paris.

"Equally helpful is research on the spot," she says. "Before writing *Guns*, I rented a little Renault and in another August drove over the battle areas of August, 1914, following the track of the German invasion through Luxembourg, Belgium and northern France. Besides obtaining a feeling of the geography, distances and terrain involved in military movements, I saw the fields ripe with grain which the cavalry would have trampled, measured the great width of the Meuse River at Liège, and saw how the lost territory of Alsace looked to the French soldiers who gazed down upon it from the heights of the Vosges Mountains."

Books establish new contacts

Bergen Evans makes an interesting point about book writing:

Basically, good book-length non-fiction establishes a writer as something of an expert in his field, giving him prestige no article is likely to. It also opens many a publishing door formerly closed to him. Books are usually bound in hard covers (publishers call them "case bound"). Therefore, they take on a permanent aspect that magazines lack. Somehow, what's written between the covers of a book seems to exude greater authority than type in a newspaper or magazine, though the words may be identical.

Books establish many new contacts for a writer, frequently leading to magazine staff jobs or article assignments, especially in the book's field. When you write a good non-fiction volume, you come to be regarded as an expert on your topic. You may qualify for lecture tours, book-and-author luncheons, even an honorary college degree.

Moreover, if you hit with a good non-fiction book, you're likely to make big money (though the percentage of best sellers is small). There are book-club and magazine condensation possibilities over and above the normal bookstore sales. Although the chances are remote, non-fiction does occasionally get sold to the movies and television, with benefits to the author. Book rights are so much a part of modern publishing that the original sale may not influence the editor to publish your book as much as its possibilities for book clubs, television, the movies, or a *Reader's Digest* condensation.

Another plus for longer non-fiction, says J.D. Ratcliff, is the fact that almost all worthy books are reviewed somewhere.

Your writing and your ideas are talked about, discussed, evaluated in public. Your prose is judged and sometimes appreciated by a vast audience which reads the reviews but seldom reads the books unless they are smash hits. Your book may sell only 5,000 copies, yet *The New York Times* Sunday book section may run your picture along with a review of your brain child and millions who never heard of you before may become aware of you as a writer.

Furthermore, there's inner satisfaction in writing a book. This can be an important and very personal thing, far above monetary reward. Seeing your first copy is at least similar to looking at a new baby in the family. One is the product of your mind, the other of your body. But both are part of *you*, and there's nothing quite so satisfying to a human being as the sense of fulfilled creation.

An alphabetical list of subjects

What kind of non-fiction book should you try? Bennett Cerf, long an editor and publisher, believes almost every writer has within him a non-fiction book that could be salable if written well. He lists these possible classes of book-length non-fiction in this alphabetical way:

agriculture	literature and criticism
biography	medicine and hygiene
business	music
education	philology
fine arts	philosophy
games and sports	poetry and drama
geography and travel	religion
history	science
home economics	sociology and economics
law	technology and military

Almost any non-fiction book can be classified under one of these headings. Gardening, for example, comes under agriculture, ethics is part of philosophy, and politics a subsection of sociology, biography or history, depending on the approach.

As to article collections and anthologies, Cerf has this to say:

The beginning writer would be wise to avoid collections and anthologies. In the first place, the anthology market has been sadly overdone in recent years. As costs of printing go up, as costs of permissions go up, anthologies have become an expensive luxury for a publishing house. They used to be so successful that publishers were receptive to anthologies. But the field has been plowed so thoroughly now that there are a dozen anthologies on every conceivable subject.

In the second place, authors have gotten tired of giving their choice bits to anthologists and their prices for reprint permissions are going up all the time. So that the anthology field is not what it used to be.

Furthermore, to be successful, an anthology must bear the name of an editor who is well-known to the public—a man who has won a big reputation in a certain field and can be counted on to do a good anthology on that subject. Without a name, an anthology today is virtually worthless.

Although almost every subject has been covered to some degree in non-fiction books, there's always room for the writer with the new slant, the fresh approach. For example, probably more words have been written about the Civil War than there were bullets fired in all the battles, and yet, books will always be written about that conflict.

Before you decide on a book subject, check reference sources to be certain that a book like the one you plan doesn't already exist.

Once you choose a subject for a proposed book, find out how many existing books relate to the same topic. At your library, search *Books in Print* for recent titles. Then look at the *Cumulative Book Index* listings for the past five years or more, noting how many and what books dealing with your subject may have been published. If there are several, a publisher may feel that the market for another would be poor—unless your idea includes some new or startling aspects.

Procure as many of the books as possible and look them over. You may find that one of them covers the same ground you had in mind. This would probably kill the sale of your manuscript, so you face a choice—either to abandon your project or see what you can do to make your book different. If a book similar to yours does not exist, then we'll assume you're encouraged enough to go ahead with the project. The next step is preliminary research.

Start with encyclopedias such as the *Britannica*, the *Americana, Collier's* and *The World Book*. These are good reference works for important details about people, places and things. Read what they have to say about your chosen subject, and for future reference make a note of authors and titles of sources in the bibliographies at the end of encyclopedia entries. Check the *Readers' Guide to Periodical Literature* for magazine articles, and search *The New York Times Index* for helpful news stories.

On the basis of the facts you uncover, you should have enough material to query a publisher about your proposed book. There are three ways to learn whether or not a publisher is interested in your idea. You can arrange a personal visit and ask him face to face, you can write a letter, or you can send an outline and sample chapters.

If you write a letter, explain carefully what the book will be about, your qualifications for writing it, and the reasons you believe it would sell. Remember, the publisher is in business to earn profits.

Probably the most effective approach is a combination of the last two ways: a letter plus an outline and sample chapters. On the basis of preliminary research, prepare a *tentative* outline and write two sample chapters. If you have to do additional research for this, do it.

Your outline needn't be in great detail. One good method is

to write a chapter outline. List your chapter numbers and headings, and under each indicate in a few sentences the substance of the content. At the top or bottom of the outline, include a brief note that this is *tentative* and may have to be revised after you've completed your research in depth.

Your preliminary research should provide enough information on which to base two sample chapters. It isn't essential that these be Chapters 1 and 2, but it's preferable. The function of the outline and sample chapters is to acquaint a prospective publisher with the significance and total content of the book, while the sample chapters reveal the quality of your work.

If he says "Yes" to your query, the publishing problem is solved. If he says "No" don't be discouraged. There may be a dozen good reasons why this publisher can't handle this particular manuscript at this particular time. Simply send the manuscript to another publisher. Send it to eight or ten—or twenty—if you have to. Some publishers will send a refusal that's little more than "No," but others will go into detail about why they have refused your manuscript. When a pattern begins to show in answers, analyze it carefully. Don't forget that a successful publisher has had plenty of experience; the reasons he gives are the results of this experience. If, say, three of them give the same reason for turning down your idea, you're looking at a red light.

What if the publisher wants you to make changes in your outline? In most cases, go ahead and make them. And for two reasons: First, he probably won't sign a contract unless you do; and second, he knows a lot more about the business than you do. One of the reasons for submitting a book in outline form is so that a publisher's changes can be incorporated into the manuscript. Mandatory changes in a completed manuscript entail rewriting, often reworking of large parts of the material.

Now, let us assume that you and a publisher have come to terms; a contract has been signed and you're ready to go ahead. What next? The sheer hard work begins. The research methods set forth in Lesson Four, although concerned with magazine articles, are just as applicable to non-fiction books. Briefly, you should:

1. Read books, magazine articles, newspaper stories, brochures or other literature pertinent to your project, making notes of helpful facts. Ask your librarian for leads.

2. Interview experts or authorities for firsthand information about your subject. Ask their permission to be quoted.

3. Write to business firms, museums, government agencies or other sources for literature or information you can use.

4. Observe activities, places or things you want to write about, if that's possible.

Here are other practical hints we've given you at different places in this Course. We're listing them again because they're just as important when you're writing a book as when you're working on an article:

1. In excerpting facts from printed materials, make complete written records of the sources—titles, names of authors, publishers, copyright dates, page numbers—for future reference.

2. To arrange for interviews with experts, make appointments in advance, either by letter or telephone, and always be on time. Follow the procedure laid down in Lesson Six on interviewing.

3. In writing to business firms and others, be as specific as you can about what you need or want, and explain why you're asking for their help.

4. In observing activities, places or things, write notes as you go. Don't try to remember what you see, for the chances are, you'll forget something important.

When do you stop researching?

This is another question that can't be answered definitely. No one person can tell another when his research is complete. Even the writer himself can't be sure until the book is finished. But in a practical sense, your outline will help you here. You can tell, roughly, when you have enough data for any specific chapter— that is, when you have perhaps twice as many facts as you think you can use. This allows you to pick and choose the best material. A chapter that doesn't have a solid backlog of facts is likely to seem thin on paper.

Use your tentative outline to help in organizing your notes and printed materials. Some authors use a file folder for each proposed chapter of a book, containing brochures, newspaper clippings, magazine articles or other literature related most directly to that chapter. The folder also holds notes pertinent to this portion of the book. When this sorting is completed, you should be able to decide whether to expand, shorten or otherwise revise your tentative outline.

Researchers bend to their quiet tasks in the Main Reading Room of the New York Public Library.

Using your final outline as a guide, you're ready now to write the first draft of your book. With a definite audience in mind, you should write directly for that audience. Your first draft may be too short to satisfy your publisher, and you may have to do more research on certain aspects. Never expand a short draft by adding words—all you're doing is writing a long version of a short book. The publisher won't like that. There's only one way to lengthen an underlength book: add more facts. Careful rewriting, revising and polishing often can make the difference between a poor and a superb book. Or even between a published book and an unpublished one.

Setting up your work schedule

Many writers, Cerf points out, work at more than one project. They appear on television panels, they lecture, perhaps they even edit books or magazines. To do this, they have to ration their time precisely, but if their writing, telecasting, editing or lecturing are related, they will do themselves professional harm only if they lack self-discipline and a logical work schedule. Cerf continues:

A lot of successful book writers rigorously set schedules for themselves. They'll work from nine o'clock in the morning until one, from three in the afternoon until eight, or some find that they can write best in the middle of the night. Once they've discovered their best working hours, they treat writing like a job and don't find a thousand excuses for delaying or postponing or changing their routine. Once you get the idea that you're going to write from nine to one each day, temperament will soon take a place in the background and you'll know that you're doing a job like everybody else. And thoughts will come to you if you train yourself to have them arrive at a regular time.

One of the things that can deeply disturb the work of a book writer is to let his life be cluttered with jobs unrelated to the main stream of his work. Writers should not allow themselves to be sucked into outside activities unless the activities are really close to their hearts. Be especially careful of people who play on your vanity to get you to assume a job you don't care about at all.

This doesn't mean you shouldn't work for, say, your community, but it should be something tied directly to your work. I would work for a library committee any day—I'll work for anything that helps writers—but I won't let myself take on jobs that aren't part of my business.

Too many people are sidetracked today by working for causes that aren't connected with the main stream of their careers. For a book writer, it's particularly important not to clutter up your life with details that only hinder you in the pursuance of your career.

Different kinds of non-fiction books

While books can be broken down into many classifications, a few *broad classes* of books should be discussed individually. They are:

1. Juvenile
2. History—Biography
3. Technical

Writing for young readers

The juvenile field has changed enormously in recent years. Formerly, juveniles sold primarily in bookstores to individual buyers and only a phenomenal best seller earned a substantial amount for its author. Today, 90 percent are sold to public libraries and schools. And because libraries replace a popular juvenile when its worn out, the author has repeat sales long after publication.

To show you how long-lived a juvenile can be, here are the titles of four books pulled at random from the shelves in the children's section of a small-town library:

Men Against Crime by John J. Floherty, 1946.
Madame Curie by Eve Curie, 1943.
Lives of Poor Boys Who Became Famous by Sarah K. Bolton, 1947.
Field Book of Common Rocks and Minerals by F. B. Loomis, 1923. (This was revised in 1948 and is currently in its twenty-fourth impression.)

A generation ago, children visited the library only occasionally; there weren't nearly as many libraries as there are now, they were harder to reach, and once you got there, the selection was probably limited. Today, the children's section may contain 20 to 30 percent or more of all the books in your local library and account for as much as half of the total circulation.

The emphasis on education has caused much of this change. Teachers use library books to enrich the program in the classroom; parents are more willing to drive their children to the library, if necessary, and there are more federal, state and local funds available for the purchase of books. Even television, which at first was condemned for keeping children from reading, has contributed to the increased demand. When something is televised that interests a child, where does he go to find out more on that particular subject? To the library, of course, for a book about it.

People outside the writing profession tend to think that writers who have found they're not capable of writing for adults turned to the juvenile field because it's easier. Nothing could be further from the truth. Writing for young readers requires great skill and a specialized knowledge of the subject you're writing

Writing for young readers
requires great skill and
a specialized knowledge
of the subject you're
writing about.

about. Young readers demand answers to their eternal "why's" and they look for the answers in books. But these books must be well researched and well written or they'll be quickly rejected.

Throughout this Course we've emphasized the principle "Know Your Audience." To write for young people, it's essential you know their requirements intimately. Start first with the age level. A book about the stars written for beginning readers is far different from one written for teen-agers, although both groups may want to know more about the subject.

Most children's books today tell on the dust jacket the age that particular book is intended for. It will give a span of several years because so much depends on the reading capability of the individual child. There are roughly four groupings, with each group overlapping another:

1. Beginning readers—kindergarten through 2nd grade—age 4 to 7
2. Middle years—3rd through 5th grades—age 8 to 10
3. Later childhood—6th through 7th or 8th—age 10 to 12
4. Young adults—junior high and high school—age 12 and up

Before you begin to write, you *must* have a clear understanding of the requirements and limitations of each group. The best advice is to go to a library and spend several days studying the books on the juvenile shelves. Talk to the librarian because she's the one the children turn to when they want to find that special book. She'll know what has already been covered completely and she may have suggestions about areas a new writer would have a chance to fill.

Talk to the teachers in your local schools, too. They may have discovered there's a need for better material on a particular subject for a particular grade level. And finally study the children's book section of your Sunday newspaper at Christmastime and in the spring when they feature juveniles. These supplements will show you the latest trends in publishing.

What subjects can you write about? There are almost no limitations: history, science, biography, the world around you or the world abroad; how-to-do-it or what-to-do. Pick almost any topic from undersea exploration to quasars, from primitive art to the signs of the zodiac and chances are that with the right approach it will be a fit subject for a juvenile book.

When you study the books in your library, you'll find the best juveniles are deceptively simple. The style is spare and uncluttered. Simple, direct words are used; if a long technical word is needed, it's always explained. Young readers are quick to perceive if the author is "writing down." They expect honest answers to their questions; answers which are complete and accurate; answers presented with imagination and enthusiasm.

Writing for any one of the different age levels can be rewarding. If young people feel that the world is their oyster, it's the non-fiction writer who cracks the shell for them.

Writing history and biography

History is another big area of non-fiction writing. There's a saying that "anybody can write history if he can do research." This is not literally true, of course, although history does "stand still" for you. The events are frozen in the records, so to speak, allowing you to take your time with research.

A major historical study, like Winston Churchill's series on World War II, is a tremendous undertaking and the province of the expert. If a new writer wanted to write a history of this war, he probably couldn't find a publisher; readers want the authority implicit in a big name. But if a new writer were content to pick a small or local phase of history, confined to a small area and a special readership, he could do very well.

Perhaps a local historical society is planning to reconstruct a Colonial village near you: you might interest them in having

The history of a reconstructed Colonial village might make an interesting subject for a book.

you write a history of the village, to be sold to visitors when the work is complete. Possibly your district had a regional hero in, say, the Revolutionary War and regular history books have passed him by. You might get local backing to underwrite all or part of a biography. You wouldn't make much money, but you would enjoy local celebrity and also have a "book in print."

If you're fortunate enough to have an attic full of letters and memorabilia left by your grandparents, you might be able to use some as the nucleus of a local history. However, there would have to be a clear bond with some famous event, series of events or with a well-known historical personality. A biography of your great uncle Henry, while it may hold family fascination, means nothing to readers.

Bruce Catton's best-selling volumes on the Civil War make him a true expert in the field of history writing. Here are some of his thoughts on the problems and techniques involved:

The very first thing in writing is to be clear in your own mind about what you want to say. I often think of my own experience in this connection. Several years ago I decided that I wanted to write about the Civil War. It seemed to me there were certain points about this war that I wanted to make—points not so much about strategy, tactics or political meanings as about the things that happen to men when they go to war, about the deep, almost incomprehensible emotional experience which this "war between brothers" brought to this country, about the deep significance underlying the whole struggle, a significance which most of the participants did not themselves understand. I wanted, in short, to have my say, and while I was fairly clear about what I wanted to say, I was not at all clear about the way I wanted to say it.

I began, or tried to begin, by writing a Civil War novel. I had a good hundred pages of this in typescript when, rereading it one morning, I realized that it was simply awful. I had chosen the wrong medium; what I wanted to say was not coming through, it was buried under a tangled assortment of words, hidden behind a set of fictitious characters who kept getting in my way and who, frankly, did not really interest me very much. So I threw away the novel and decided that I would simply write a narrative about a certain period in the career of one of the armies in that war.

It turned out, in the end, that I was writing history, although the idea never entered my head at the time. My only advantage was that I did know what I wanted to say, and that I realized in time I lacked the novelist's talents.

What all of this means perhaps is that what you want to say may in the end determine how you say it. In other words, the content of what you write dictates the form in which you write it. And that form, for me, turns out to be non-fiction.

The writing of technical books

The technical book, since it's far longer than an article for a technical magazine or trade publication, is a taxing assignment for a writer, beginner or professional. But the rewards are in proportion to the extra work, for a good technical book (brought up to date every few years) is the equivalent, in royalties, of an endowment insurance policy. Prestige is another factor in favor of technical books compared with technical articles.

Let's examine the kinds of technical books that engineers, scientists, technicians and informed journalists write and find a good market for. There are many types, but they can be roughly classed in six categories: (1) technical training texts, (2) college technical texts, (3) industrial reference books, (4) advanced engineering books, (5) engineering monographs, and (6) handbooks. Let's look at each.

1. *Technical training texts.* Often a text of this type is prepared for study by candidates training for technician-level jobs in industry. These are usually high-school graduates having the fundamental training in physics and chemistry given in secondary schools.

Good technical training texts are characterized by clear, simple writing, combined with careful matching of text and illustrations. These characteristics are desirable in every technical book; however, the extra effort you make to produce an outstanding technical training text is appreciated by all readers.

2. *College technical texts.* These are most frequently written by teachers in engineering schools and by part-time faculty members. Relatively few engineers and technicians in industry can write a text specifically for use in colleges. Most books of this type are also of interest to engineers in the field, and are usually written for them. But some of the books written by engineers in industry are adopted later as college texts. Keep these facts in mind when you think about writing a text for college use.

Occasionally college texts are co-authored by an engineer on

the teaching staff and an engineer in industry. Each contributes his particular talent and knowledge to produce well-balanced coverage. Collaborating with a teacher is probably the best way for you to write a college text if you are not a faculty member yourself.

3. *Industrial reference books*. These are written primarily for engineers, scientists and technicians working in a particular field. They may also be used by students, salesmen, technicians and others interested in that field. If you study a number of industrial reference books, you will see that this type puts somewhat more emphasis on application than on theory. The man in the field is more interested in solution of problems related to his job. Theoretical discussions are of little use to him unless he can see some relation between them and his daily work.

4. *Advanced engineering books*. These differ from industrial reference books in a number of ways. In general, the advanced engineering book is more theoretical. It is directed at a higher audience level and is likely to have a mathematical approach. The subject matter generally deals more with design and engineering considerations than with the problems of installation, operation and maintenance. There are, of course, some variations in these characteristics, but they are typical of many advanced engineering books today. Keep these in mind when you think of writing an advanced engineering book.

5. *Engineering monographs*. These books usually cover a limited area of a particular field. Instead of giving a broad view of the field, as some industrial reference books do, the usual engineering monograph delves deeply, but over a restricted area. A mathematical approach is commonly used. The mathematics may be more rigorous than in an advanced engineering book.

6. *Handbooks*. These are not "written" in the same sense as most other technical books are. Instead, there are a number of contributors, often more than 50, each of whom writes a portion or section of the book. These sections are submitted to the editor of the handbook, who works the material into unified coverage of the subject matter. To achieve this, the editor may restyle

Books on advanced engineering generally deal more with design and engineering considerations, like those involved with this huge atomic reactor, than with problems of installation and operation.

some of the material submitted but he never alters its factual content. When the editor is a specialist in some phase of a field, as is often the case, he may write one or more sections of the handbook himself.

In many ways, editing a handbook is the ultimate in technical craftsmanship. But you must have long experience in your profession and a high degree of writing skill before you can qualify for the task. A wide acquaintance with the outstanding members of the profession covered by the handbook is another necessity— if a large number of contributors is contemplated.

How to write a sleeper

A suitable ending for this Lesson on writing non-fiction books comes from Rudolf Flesch, a member of our Guiding Faculty who has a special gift for writing best sellers. In an article for the *Famous Writers Magazine,* he gives some sound rules to follow if you want to turn out a "trivial" book that some day could become No. 1 on the book-buyers' list.

A sleeper, according to Webster's Third Unabridged Dictionary (definition 7c), is "a book that sells well year after year without being advertised." This definition covers a wide variety of books: *Who's Who in America* and *The Prophet* by Kahlil Gibran; Emily Post's *Etiquette* and A. A. Milne's *Winnie-the-Pooh*; Robert's *Rules of Order* and Mrs. Irma Rombauer's *New Joy of Cooking*; *The Story of Philosophy* by Will Durant; *The Outline of History* by H. G. Wells; Thoreau's *Walden*; Samuel Butler's *Erewhon*; *Alice in Wonderland*; *The Rubaiyat*; *Peter Rabbit*.

What do all these books have in common? Is there any underlying principle, any secret that makes a book into a perennial seller? Oddly enough, the answer is yes. Go through the titles I've listed and you'll find that each one of them became a hidden best seller because *it was not meant to be one*. A sleeper, by its very nature, is a book that astonishes both author and publisher by its enduring success.

Who's Who started as a modest list of notables drawn up by a 19th-century English journalist—a sort of private "morgue." Emily Post's *Etiquette* came into being because Mrs. Post was a well-brought-up society matron who put down on paper what she knew about good manners. A. A. Milne had had success with a mystery novel and had gotten a sizeable advance on another one. So—human nature being what it is—he shirked the job and filled his time by making up little verses for his small son.

Will Durant wrote his essays on various philosophers for the famous five-cent Little Blue Books; the book that was later made out of them was an afterthought. H. G. Wells was world-famous for his novels and scientific romances; his publisher discouraged him heartily when he came up with the idea of writing a one-volume world history. Thoreau went to Walden Pond to seek solitude, not to write a book.

Lewis Carroll was a mathematician who spent an evening spinning a long yarn for two little girls and was prevailed upon to write it down. Edward Fitzgerald was a student of Oriental literature who for his own interest and amusement translated Omar Khayyam's epigrams; when a bookseller offered some of his unsalable copies for a penny apiece, the poet, Dante Gabriel Rossetti, picked one up and made *The Rubaiyat* famous.

I can add two experiences of my own to this illustrious catalogue. I wrote my first book, *The Art of Plain Talk*, because I'd become absorbed in the subject of my doctor's thesis—the scientific study of readability. I made it into a book for the general public, offered it to a publisher and was promptly turned down. Then I went to a second publisher, who gingerly decided to pay me a small advance and print 2,000 copies. When the book came out, people in the professional writing field discovered it had something in it. It has sold steadily for 17 years.

Another sleeper, *Why Johnny Can't Read*, started when a friend and neighbor told me her 12-year-old son couldn't read. I spent some months teaching him, then decided to turn my experience into a book.

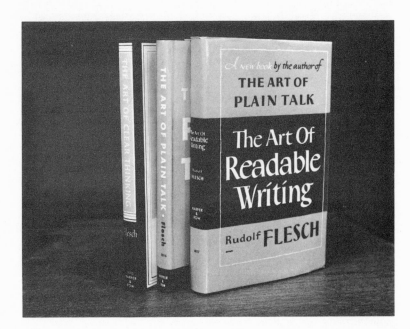

Rudolf Flesch has a knack for writing sleepers—books which surprisingly become perennial best sellers.

When I offered it to my publisher, he was extremely bearish on the project and tried his best to discourage me. Finally he published it anyway. It became a best seller at once and after a year or two it turned into a regular bookstore perennial.

What's the moral of all these little tales? Simply this: If you want to write a sleeper, don't go at it directly. Pursue a hobby; bury yourself in some unpromising activity, do a job for the love of it; get absorbed in something that offers no financial reward whatever; swim against the current of fashionable, best-selling writing; and perhaps you'll succeed.

Begin by knowing all there is to know about hooked rugs; or cooking with wine; or collecting a paperback library; or basket weaving; or making doll clothes; or winning at Scrabble. Then, when your accumulated experience cries out for making itself known, start on your own book.

And now let's assume you've reached the point of writing it. How do you proceed? What kind of book are you going to write? Should it be long or short? How should it be arranged? What should go in and what should be left out? What's the proper technique of packaging a useful, humble, unglamorous sort of book?

Let's begin with the question of the proper size. The answer to this one is simple: If your book is destined to become a sleeper, it will start small and gradually grow until it has reached natural length. In its first version it will naturally contain everything you've learned in your intense preoccupation with the subject; in later revisions it will slowly thicken because by then you'll have become a book author who's keeping up with his chosen field.

Generally speaking, all established dictionaries, encyclopedias, cookbooks, manuals, guidebooks and how-to-live books have this tendency to grow over the years. However, there are exceptions. Sometimes an author writes a little book that becomes a sleeper and is then compelled to write another one like it—and a third—and a fourth. A.A. Milne's *Winnie-the-Pooh* books are such a series, and Beatrix Potter's *Peter Rabbit* books and Arnold Bennett's successive volumes of pocket philosophy. Essentially, though, these cases are just variations upon the basic theme; in the end the sleeper emerges as the sum total of the series of little books, or perhaps as an omnibus volume, like Arnold Bennett's *How to Live on 24 Hours a Day*. (My own books on writing eventually became a combination package entitled *How to Write, Speak and Think More Effectively*.)

If you offer your book to the world in too small a format, it simply won't have enough body to become a perennial seller. Emile Coué's *Self-Mastery Through Conscious Autosuggestion* takes up just 24 pages. There is a brief volume called *Better and Better Every Day*, which contains Coué's original manuscript plus some other connected material, but it was never substantial enough to make a permanent place for itself in the bookstores.

H.L. Mencken was an author who let his books grow too long. His *American Language* started as a normal-size book but eventually became a monster treatise in three enormous volumes. His *New Dictionary of Quotations* started out as a simple collection of his own favorite quotations; then, midstream in preparing the book, Mencken was bitten by the bug of all-inclusiveness and turned the book into a 1,347-page catchall for every proverb, quote and wise saying he could lay his hands on.

So make your book neither too short nor too long. Next question: How should the material be arranged? Do you serve up the dishes in your cookbook proceeding from breakfast to dinner and from soup to nuts? Or do you start by teaching the young bride how to boil an egg and wind up showing the sophisticated hostess how to serve a perfect baked Alaska? Do you go from the inexpensive to the expensive? Or from the quick to the slow?

Again, my advice is to let things take their natural course. Your own mastery of the subject will suggest the best way of presenting it to others. You yourself will have some reference books that make you feel at home and some others that exasperate you every time you have to use them.

Often—far more than you'd think—the best arrangement to fall back on is the good old alphabet. After all, if a book is arranged according to the ABC method, the reader can always get at everything he wants with one familiar motion. Don't think the ABC arrangement is stupid, illogical, arbitrary; of course it is, but no plan of your own can possibly beat it for sheer convenience. Remember that Fowler's *Modern English Usage* existed first as the topically arranged *The King's English*; when it had settled down to a life of its own as one of the world's finest sleepers, Fowler had to do the whole job over again by making it into an alphabetical dictionary.

Similarly, Roget's *Thesaurus*—with its highly original scheme of categories— went through edition after edition until in the end the index more or less swallowed up the text. And J.K. Lasser's *Your Income Tax* adds new alphabetical check lists every year.

If you do adopt an alphabetical scheme as the basic pattern of your book, you'll earn an unexpected reward: it will make your job immeasurably easier. I'll never forget the moment when I got around to the final preparation of the manuscript of my book *How to Be Brief*. Up to then I had written all my books on writing in the standard fashion—an introductory chapter followed by the first topic to be discussed, then the second, then the third, and so on. Suddenly I realized that with the alphabetical scheme I had freed myself of all the labor of devising introductions, leads, transitions, logical sequences, any kind of structural device. I put a large A on the first page of my manuscript and there I was—my book had arranged itself.

Find the right size, then find the right arrangement. Next, find the secret ingredient—the formula, the gimmick, the thing readers will remember as the essence of your book. To sell "year after year without advertising," your book will have to have something about it that will make people recommend it to one another across dinner tables and back fences.

Is your book a guide to world literature? Make it into a list of the Hundred Best Books. Are you writing about traveling in Europe? Work out one-week, two-week, three-week tours. Do you have a new diet to offer? Give them meal plans with fixed calorie counts.

Don't despise people's craving for the neatly labeled package, the formula, the memory aid. That's just the way the human mind works —your own, too. As the author of a sleeper, you're in the business of giving people a handy service; make it as easy as possible for them to assimilate what's in your book.

I learned about this principle the hard way. My first book, *The Art of Plain Talk*, contained a formula to measure readability; among other things people had to count the number of affixes (prefixes and suffixes) within 100 words. After a year or two I realized I'd asked people for too much work; so I sat down during weeks and weeks of a hot summer and refigured all my original statistics to make people count syllables instead of affixes. The change made the formula less accurate, but vastly more acceptable to the public.

The useful-book author's work is never done. The years go by, the book sells on and on, readers keep writing in and your files grow and grow. You revise the text, you add material, you weed out what's obsolete. The book gets older, but there are nice things about an old book, too. Some passages begin to seem quaint; some features take on an historical flavor. But readers like it that way, and you get letters from Montana or Israel or Alaska, thanking you enthusiastically for something you wrote five, ten, twenty years ago.

It's a good life. Somehow, like gardening or puttering in a basement workshop, it seems to make for a long, peaceful old age. I have no definitive research finds to offer, but I do know that Sir George Grove, editor of the *Dictionary of Music and Musicians*, lived to be 80; Burton Stevenson, compiler of *The Home Book of Quotations*, died at 90; John Bartlett of *Bartlett's Familiar Quotations*, died at 85; Peter Mark Roget died at 90; Liberty Hyde Bailey, editor of the *Standard Cyclopedia of Horticulture*, died at 96. And Thomas à Kempis, who wrote the most venerable sleeper of them all, *The Imitation of Christ*, ended his saintly life at the age of 91.

Those who don't know, of course, will say that the long life of the dictionary or handbook author must be unbearably dull. But they're wrong. Some years ago a friend found me immersed in the thousands of little index cards that eventually made up my *Book of Unusual Quotations*. I told him I'd been at it for six solid months.

Sympathetically he said, "I bet you'll be happy when you're through with this dull job."

Dull? The idea startled me. I thought the job was fascinating.

"Some years ago a friend found me immersed in the thousands of little index cards that eventually made up my *Book of Unusual Quotations...."*

Perhaps you'll never write a sleeper—or, indeed, any kind of book. Perhaps you'll never even attempt one. Dollar for dollar, your decision to concentrate on shorter material may be wise. For most professional writers, there is probably more money to be made in articles than in books.

Yet, there is a special satisfaction in writing a book. Books have permanence and prestige that articles cannot have. They broaden a writer's horizons and open up new contacts. Then, there is always that attractive chance of hitting with a best seller, which means fame and money. Or your book may highlight an important issue to millions of thoughtful people and bring about much-needed reform.

This can be the best reward of all.

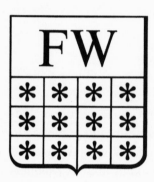

Reading
for
writing

Volume IV

As in Volume III of this Non-Fiction Course, we are including two articles written by professional authors and published in
magazines of general interest. For Volume IV we have selected
"The Lure of Roses" by Dorothy H. Jenkins, and "A Madness
of Nature" by Franklin Russell.

Once more, the articles differ in style, tone and subject matter—and are worthwhile examples of non-fiction as it is written
and published today. We have reprinted the articles so that the
lefthand page contains our editorial comments while the right-
hand page contains the text.

We suggest that you read the articles from beginning to end to
understand thoroughly their subject and scope. Then, go back
to the beginning and read the articles through with reference to
our comments. In this way, we feel you will derive great value
from these pieces as examples of work to guide you while doing
work of your own.

By Dorothy H. Jenkins

The
lure of
roses

This *Woman's Day* article is an example of the kind of
piece that can develop out of a hobby.
The subject is roses, their history and habits, and the
author is a woman whose garden
has long been the envy of friends and neighbors.

Roses, those irresistibly attractive flowers, have charmed
people throughout the ages, so much so that flower lovers have
carried them great distances, the better to enjoy and share them.
Many centuries ago the Crusaders took the sweetly fragrant
Rose of Damascus from the Holy Land to Europe and England,
while during the nineteenth century American pioneers found
room in their wagons for slips of Harison's Yellow roses to be
planted in their new homes in the West.

Species roses, such as the Rose of Damascus, and the garden
varieties that sprang from them are all classed as old-fashioned
or old roses. They comprise a group as diverse in their habit of
growth as in the size, shape and color of the flowers. Their most

"The Lure of Roses" is typical of many articles
in consumer-service magazines like
Woman's Day, intended as much to give
information as to entertain. Consequently, the
writer must be sure to organize the article
thoughtfully and carefully—in other words, to
outline before beginning to write.

After the lead and a brief discussion of
miniature roses, the author moves into the body of
the article. Here we see the organization of
the piece emerging. She has chosen to develop her
discussion of roses around Empress Josephine's
famous rose garden at Malmaison, France. The
choice is a logical one since the garden
contained species of all the known old roses.

striking common characteristic is fragrance, and until a person has sniffed a damask or a cabbage rose, it is impossible to imagine true rose fragrance.

The first miniature rose was brought to England from the island of Mauritius about 1810. It was named *Rosa lawranceana* in honor of Mary Lawrance, a well-known painter of flowers. Miss Lawrance's rose—about six inches tall with semidouble pale pink flowers no larger than the tip of a little finger—is believed to have been brought to America early in the nineteenth century, although until recently this type was never so popular here as in England. Both there and here the popularity of miniature roses diminished around 1870.

Then, in the 1920's, a miniature rose with double rose-pink flowers, now called *Rosa rouletti,* was discovered as a pot plant in Switzerland and introduced to the rest of the rose world. Since then, many new varieties have been introduced to this country under such delightful names as Cinderella, Scarlet Gem, Sweet Fairy, Tinker Belle and Red Imp.

The original *Rosa lawranceana,* with pale pink flowers, undoubtedly was included in the famous rose garden that the Empress Josephine planted at Malmaison in the early years of the nineteenth century. For her star-shaped garden enclosed by avenues of lime trees, Josephine assembled all the known roses of her day—about 250 species and varieties. Most of them flowered only once each year, but a few were remontant, meaning that they flowered heavily in June and bloomed lightly about once a month thereafter during the season.

White roses of all kinds were Josephine's favorites, so she must have loved the richly fragrant white damask rose named Unique; the climbing ivory musk roses with their special scent; the larger-flowering climbing Cherokee; pure white and blush varieties of English *Rosa alba*; and the almost white, monthly flowering *Rosa indica,* known as the China, or Bengal, rose. Of course, there was a delightfully scented hybrid named Empress Josephine; when open, it displayed silvery pink petals shading to deeper pink at the center, and each petal was veined with an even deeper tone of pink.

The garden at Malmaison did more than gratify Josephine's passionate love of roses. One great legacy is the portraits by Pierre-Joseph Redouté, "the Raphael of flowers," for which

One sign of a skilled non-fiction writer is the
ability to weave interesting extra facts
into the manuscript without disturbing the flow of
the piece or straying too far from the
central, unifying thought. An example (there
are others which you'll detect as you go
along) is the brief discussion of the Redouté
rose portraits.

In our introduction, we noted that this is an article
which could develop from a hobby.
Considering both the kind and the amount of
information in the piece—information
almost beyond the scope of research—it is unlikely
that it could have been written by someone
other than a person with an intimate knowledge
of the subject.

Another of those interesting extra facts—several
of them in a single sentence, to be exact.
These tidbits of information about the Apothecary
rose bring color and variety to the piece and
make it livelier reading.

her roses were models. *Les Roses,* with some 200 Redouté color plates and text by C.A. Thory, is still considered an outstanding achievement. No one has ever captured the grace, charm and distinguishing characteristics of roses as well as Redouté, and some of his portraits show such delicacy that one can almost feel the silken texture of the petals and imagine their perfume.

Josephine was a true patroness of her favorite flower for she made rose-growing fashionable and influenced botanists, nurserymen and gardeners of her time not only to grow roses but also to hybridize in order to obtain new and improved varieties. In 1937, the late Dr. J.H. Nicolas, noted rose hybridist, estimated that 16,000 varieties of roses had appeared since 1810. All of them, in a way, are a tribute to Josephine.

Nine varieties of damask roses that were grown in Europe between 1600 and about 1875 were planted at Malmaison. The original Rose of Damascus opened intensely fragrant double pink flowers, usually in clusters of three or more. Of the many famous varieties, none has been enjoyed by more people, if only secondhand, than Kazanlik. It has been cultivated for centuries in the Balkans, where its richly scented bright rose-pink petals are still gathered to make attar of roses.

Fully as ancient a variety is Rose of Castile, which must have been taken to California in the seventeenth or eighteenth century by the Spanish. Its semidouble light pink flowers are followed by scarlet hips. One of its charms for people on the West Coast who still grow it is its tendency to repeat bloom. Virgil, who knew a remontant damask as the Rose of Paestum or the Pompeii rose, alluded to it as the rose that had "a double spring."

The greatest number of any one kind of rose in the Empress Josephine's garden was 107 varieties of *Rosa gallica,* noted for their many colors and sharp, sweet perfume. The Apothecary rose, sometimes wrongly called the Red Damask, was one of the first kinds brought to America by the settlers, who prized it for both its beauty and its medicinal virtues, such as easing a cough and "comforting the heart." The sizable flat flowers of the Apothecary rose, usually consisting of about twelve petals opening to show yellow stamens, were rose-red with an undertone of magenta. *Rosa gallica* had a strong tendency to produce varieties with striped or spotted flowers. Best known of all is the one grown in English gardens since the twelfth century as *Rosa*

While it is important to vary sentence openings in
every kind of writing, it is especially
important in a piece as heavily detailed and fact-
filled as this. It is also probably more
difficult to do. But the author handles it throughout
with skill and apparent ease.

In line with the comment above, notice the simple
but highly effective variety of sentence
openings in this paragraph, as well as in all the
others on the facing page.

mundi, named for its association with Fair Rosamund, mistress of Henry II.

Fewer varieties were created of *Rosa centifolia,* "the rose with a hundred petals," perhaps because people thought this lovely double pink rose could not be improved upon. It flowered in the gardens of Midas, King of Phrygia, "surpassing all others in fragrance." It is believed to have been brought to America, where it has generally been called the cabbage rose, in the 1620's. The name isn't flattering, but it is descriptive of the globular flowers, whose petals overlap like the leaves of a cabbage. The cabbage rose has always been a favorite of painters and is likely to be the rose in those lush bouquets painted by old Dutch masters.

A spontaneous variation of the cabbage rose was appropriately named moss rose. It inherited the ineffable fragrance of its parent and is distinguished by a mossy projection on the long green sepals that enclose the bud. This fragrant, rather sticky "moss" extends along the stem, too. There is nothing common about the Common Moss rose, which has long, flaring, mossy green sepals around double pink flowers and was noted first before 1600.

Crested Moss, also known as Chapeau de Napoleon and introduced in 1827, has bright pink flowers and sepals so mossy that they are like green velvet. Moss roses reached their height of popularity in the 1830's and 1840's when each year as many as 100 new varieties were originated in France. These named varieties produced quaint and rather small double flowers in white and shades of pink and red. A number of these nineteenth-century varieties flower heavily in June and less heavily periodically during the summer. Perhaps as many as a dozen of the old varieties can still be purchased for planting.

Only a few yellow roses were available for the original garden at Malmaison. One was the round, double, bright yellow Sulphur rose, which had reached France from Turkey in 1629. Yellow roses were indigenous to Turkey, Iran and the Near East and were not known in Europe until the Moors took them to Spain in the thirteenth century. Every yellow rose grown today is descended somehow or other from the yellow rose species native to the Near East. Austrian Brier, or Austrian Yellow, and Austrian Copper, despite their names, came from the hillsides

Gradually, almost imperceptibly, the author moves
from a discussion of old roses, many of which
are rarely grown nowadays, into a consideration of
those varieties which may be found in
modern gardens.

The transfer of emphasis from old roses to new
is still under way. More and more,
modern varieties find their way into the text.

of Asia Minor, but were taken to northern Europe from Austria. Harison's Yellow originated in a garden in New York City in the 1820's and caught people's fancy so quickly that a trail of this easy-to-grow variety was planted across the United States during the Westward migration.

One of the parents of Harison's Yellow must have been the shrubby, thorny Scotch rose (*Rosa spinoissima*). Both Harison's Yellow and Stanwell Perpetual, a spontaneous hybrid of the Scotch rose, flower in my garden in June. More people nowadays grow Scotch rose hybrids introduced since 1940. Two of the finest are Frühlingsgold, with large single golden blossoms, and Frühlingsmorgen, with similar flowers that are cherry-pink around each creamy center.

It is still possible to buy the English sweetbrier, or eglantine, widely grown in the time of England's Queen Elizabeth I. Long before its small light pink or white flowers open, eglantine perfumes the garden with the apple scent of its leaflets. This is particularly noticeable after a rain or heavy dew.

A few other favorites of past centuries are still being grown in regions where the climate is mild. Popular in the Southwest is the ever-blooming climber Maréchal Niel, whose round brilliant yellow flowers have a distinct and pleasing fragrance. When it was introduced in 1864, Maréchal Niel represented a great advance in the development of yellow garden roses. The climbing Cherokee, the official state flower of Georgia, has been growing so long in America that no one knows exactly how or when it reached here.

Cherokee derives from the Chinese *Rosa laevigata,* which the English East India Company took to Europe before 1696. There are a pink and a semidouble white Cherokee, but the one most loved has large single white flowers centered with golden stamens. Also from China by way of England are the Lady Banks climbers that start flowering in March in the Southeast and Southwest.

Most common are the white variety, with a violet scent, and a pale yellow; both open their flowers in clusters like cherry blossoms on thornless stems. Then there are the Old Blush and Hermosa varieties of the China, or Bengal rose. Old Blush, also called Old Pink Monthly, opens its gracefully formed and delicately shaded flowers every month of the year in some California

Here the author takes up the hybrid tea rose, the
most popular and widely grown modern
garden rose, and the move from old roses to new is
complete. It has not been accidental,
of course. Far from it. The shift in emphasis
couldn't have been made so smoothly had it not
been planned and detailed in advance—
another example of an outline working to the
author's advantage.

gardens. This was the rose which the poet Thomas Moore was thinking of when he wrote "The Last Rose of Summer."

Most famous of all hybrid perpetual roses in the United States was the one called American Beauty. It was introduced as Mme. Ferdinand Jamin in 1875 in France, where it was bred. When brought to this country in 1882, it was renamed American Beauty. The name, rather than the flower itself, made this variety a legend. It never proved satisfactory to grow in American gardens, but its long-stemmed, many-petaled and extremely fragrant flowers of carmine-pink could be grown to perfection under glass as a florist's cut flower. It was grown under glass everywhere in this country from about 1900 to 1929, when it began to be supplanted by newer and more vigorous varieties of similar or better color.

The poor performance of the European-bred American Beauty rose in American gardens provides a capsule explanation of why hybridizing of new varieties was finally undertaken here. Many fine new varieties still come from Europe, but now they are often equalled and sometimes surpassed by American-bred roses. The first American introductions were in the new hybrid tea class, which became the most widely grown type of garden rose during the first half of the twentieth century. Europeans started the work toward hybrid teas by making crosses between the tea rose of China and India and the hybrid perpetual developed in Europe.

The first hybrid tea, in 1867, was the appropriately named La France, with fragrant pink flowers. As we know hybrid teas today, the bushes have an average height of three feet and several main stems, or canes, on which magnificent flowers open repeatedly. Their size depends on the number of petals; their shape and form depend on their ancestry. Of the innumerable varieties, some are finer than others and a few perform best only in certain regions.

Crimson Glory from Germany, 1935, is a classic red hybrid tea with large, fragrant, rich dark red blossoms that are hard to beat. For a time, hybridists seemed to have become so interested in the qualities of color and constant bloom that many varieties had only the merest trace of any rose scent. A studied effort to produce more fragrant hybrid teas has brought, in the last ten years or so, varieties offering a range of rose scents.

Two more modern rose varieties, floribundas and grandifloras, receive attention before the author returns briefly to old roses to close her piece. She ends with mixed feelings of sadness and joy—sadness that true old roses are no longer popular, joy that at least she still has a few in her garden "to sniff and admire."

Easier to grow and requiring less care than hybrid teas are the two contemporary groups, floribunda and grandiflora. True to their name, floribunda varieties flower abundantly and constantly from May or June to November. Flowers, single or double, large or small, open in clusters.

The first floribundas appeared in the late 1930's. Then in 1954 came crimson-flowering Carrousel, the first grandiflora. Grandiflora roses are an American development tailored to fit the following definition, written by hybridist H.C. Swim: "Modern rosebushes must give a good display of flowers for months instead of only during June, provide flowers of medium size on stems long enough for cutting, and require minimum care." It is met by every one of the two dozen or so grandiflora varieties.

In spite of their charm, true old roses do not belong in every backyard today. Varieties of damask, cabbage and gallica roses, the mainstay of gardens until well along in the nineteenth century, do not meet the standards of today's gardeners and homeowners. Their flowers may be lovely and different, but most of them bloom only once a year. Many are susceptible to diseases, and some take considerable knowledge of rose care to have them perform well. However, it wouldn't seem like June to me without Stanwell Perpetual, Common Moss and a nameless pink cabbage rose to sniff and admire to my heart's content.

About the author

For fourteen years Dorothy H. Jenkins served as a garden editor of *The New York Times*. Currently she is antiques editor of *Woman's Day*. Her books and articles are devoted almost exclusively to these two subjects.

By Franklin Russell

A madness
of
nature

From *New American Review* comes this remarkable
article by a most accomplished
nature writer. It represents not only the best
in nature writing but also the best in
non-fiction written for a high-quality market.

Beyond the northern beach, a gray swell rolls in from Greenland and runs softly along the shore. The horizon is lost in a
world of gray, and gulls glide, spectral in the livid air. Watching,
I am enveloped in the sullen waiting time and feel the silence,
drawn out long and thin. I wait for the sea to reveal a part of
itself.

A capelin is perhaps the best-hunted creature on earth. It is
not more than five inches long, about the size of a young herring,
and undistinguished in appearance, except that when it is freshly
caught, it is the color of mercury. As the capelin dies, its silvery
scales tarnish and the glitter goes out like a light, ending a small
allegory about nature, a spectacle of victims, victors, and an

There is, of course, natural drama in the subject of
this article—a little fish "born to be eaten,"
born to die. But the author heightens the drama
through his masterful use of language.
Every word is carefully chosen, every phrase
carefully worked and reworked. The
result is prose with the lush, rhythmic feel of poetry.

By telling his story in first-person present tense,
the author adds still further to the dramatic
impact. "I see them . . . I follow them . . . I have
come to see their rush for eternity." Here
the writer is not—as in so many pieces—an
impersonal narrator. Rather, he is totally, actively
involved in the events taking place. And
so is the reader.

imperative of existence. Its death illuminates a dark process of biology in which there are shadows of other, more complex lives.

The capelin are born to be eaten. They transform oceanic plankton into flesh which is then hunted greedily by almost every sea creature that swims or flies. Their only protection is fecundity. One capelin survives to adulthood from every ten thousand eggs, yet a single school may stir square miles of sea.

In mid-June, the capelin gather offshore. They can be seen everywhere and at all times in history, symbols of summer and fertility, of Providence and danger. I see them along the shores of Greenland, Iceland, Norway, and near Spitsbergen. I follow them across the northern coast of Russia. Chill air, gray seas, the northern silence are the capelin's world in Alaska, in the Aleutians, around Hudson Bay, and along the northeastern shores of North America. But the capelin of the Newfoundland coast are the most visible. Here, they spawn on the beaches rather than in deep water offshore, and I have come to see their rush for eternity.

They gather a thousand feet offshore, coalescing into groups of a hundred thousand to break the water's surface with bright chuckling sounds. They gather, and grow. Soon they are in the millions, with other millions swimming up from the offshore deeps. They gather, now in the billions, so densely packed together in places the sea shimmers silver for miles and flows, serpentine, with the swelling body of a single, composite creature.

The fish do, in fact, possess a common sense of purpose. Nothing can redirect their imperative to breed. I once swam among them and saw them parting reluctantly ahead of me, felt their bodies flicking against my hands. Looking back, I saw them closing in, filling up the space created by my passage. The passive fish tolerated me, in their anticipation of what they were about to do.

At this time of the year they are so engrossed that they barely react when a host of creatures advances to kill them. Beneath and beyond them, codfish pour up out of the deep. They overtake the capelin, eat them, plunge their sleek, dark bodies recklessly into shallow water. Some have swum so rapidly from such depths that their swim bladders are distended by the sudden drop in water pressure. The cod are gigantic by comparison with the capelin. Many weigh one hundred pounds or more, and

Strong verbs are the backbone of strong
sentences. That statement has seldom been better
illustrated than in this article. Look at the lively,
colorful verbs on this page alone. "The
water *writhes* with movement . . . cod *drive*
themselves clear out of the sea . . . jaws
rip and *tear* . . . *taxi* with fluttering wings . . . each
bird *pumps* forward . . . " Verbs like these
make a story vital and exciting. Used in the present
tense, as they are here, they bring an
immediacy to the piece that makes it even more
exciting. The action is here and now—happening
as you read.

will not be sated until they have eaten scores of capelin each. The water writhes with movement and foam where cod, head-long in pursuit, drive themselves clear out of the sea and fall back with staccato slaps.

The attack of the codfish is a brutal opening to a ritual, and a contradiction in their character. Normally, they are sedentary feeders on the sea floor. Now, however, they are possessed. Their jaws rip and tear; the water darkens with capelin blood; shredded pieces of flesh hang suspended or rise to the surface.

Now a group of seabirds, the parrotlike puffins, clumsy in flight, turn over the capelin, their grotesque, axlike beaks prob-ing from side to side as they watch the upper layers of the mas-sacre. They are joined by new formations of birds until several thousand puffins are circling. They are silent, and there is no way of knowing how they were summoned from their nesting burrows on an island that is out of sight. They glide down to the water—stub-winged cargo planes—land awkwardly, taxi with fluttering wings and stamping paddle feet, then dive.

At the same time, the sea view moves with new invasions of seabirds. Each bird pumps forward with an urgency that sug-gests it has received the same stimulus as the cod. The gulls that breed on cliffs along a southern bay come first, gracefully light of wing, with raucous voice as they cry out their anticipation. Beneath them, flying flat, direct, silent, come murres, black-bodied, short-tailed, close relatives of the puffins. The murres land and dive without ceremony. Well offshore, as though wait-ing confirmation of the feast, shearwaters from Tristan da Cunha turn long, pointed wings across the troughs of waves and cackle like poultry.

The birds converge, and lose their identity in the mass thick-ening on the water. Small gulls—kittiwakes, delicate in flight—screech and drop and rise and screech and drop like snow-flakes on the sea. They fall among even smaller birds, lighter than they, which dangle their feet and hover at the water's sur-face, almost walking on water as they seek tiny pieces of shredded flesh. These are the ocean-flying petrels, the Mother Carey's chickens of mariners' legends, which rarely come within sight of land. All order is lost in the shrieking tumult of the hundreds of thousands of birds.

Underwater, the hunters meet among their prey. The puffins

As we said earlier, the author's prose reads like
poetry. "Silver walls of capelin flicker,
part, re-form . . ." This simple yet highly evocative
sentence is an example.

"The seals rise, well beyond the tumult of the
seabirds . . ." Another sentence
that bears the touch of the poet.

And another. Actually, there are few sentences
in this article that don't have at
least an expression with the ring of poetry.

and murres dive below the capelin and attack, driving for the surface. The cod attack at mid-depth. The gulls smother the surface and press the capelin back among the submarine hunters. The murres and puffins fly underwater, their beating wings turning them rapidly back and forth. They meet the cod, flail wings in desperate haste, are caught, crushed, and swallowed. Now seabirds as well as capelin become the hunted. Puffin and murre tangle wings. Silver walls of capelin flicker, part, re-form. Some seabirds surface abruptly, broken wings dangling. Others, with a leg or legs torn off, fly frantically, crash, skitter in shock across the water.

I see the capelin hunters spread across the sea, but also remember them in time. Each year the hunters are different because many of them depend on a fortuitous meeting with their prey. A group of small whales collides with the capelin, and in a flurry of movement they eat several tons of them. Salmon throw themselves among the capelin with the same abandon as the codfish, and in the melee become easy victims for a score of seals that kill dozens of them, then turn to the capelin and gorge themselves nearly stuporous. The seals rise, well beyond the tumult of the seabirds, their black heads jutting like rocks from the swell, to lie with distended bellies and doze away their feast. Capelin boil up around them for a moment but now the animals ignore their bounty.

The capelin are hosts in a ceremony so ancient that a multitude of species have adapted to seeking a separate share of the host's bounty. The riotous collision of cod, seal, whale, and seabird obscures the smaller guests at the feast. Near the shore wait small brown fish—the cunner—one of the most voracious species. Soon they will be fighting among themselves for pieces of flesh as the capelin begin their run for the beach, or when the survivors of the spawning reel back into deep water, with the dead and dying falling to the bottom. If the water is calm and the sun bright, the cunner can be seen in two fathoms, ripping capelin corpses to pieces and scattering translucent scales like silver leaves in a wind of the sea.

Closer inshore, at the wave line, the flounder wait. They know the capelin are coming and their role is also predetermined. They cruise rapidly under the purling water in uncharacteristic excitement. They are not interested in capelin flesh. They want

Throughout the piece the author uses repeated
words and phrases to good effect. In the
foregoing paragraph, every sentence except the first
begins with the pronoun *they*. "They
know . . . They cruise . . . They are not interested . . .
They want . . ." The feeling created through
the repetition tells of the flounder's relentless,
predestined drive for capelin eggs far
better than mere words.

Again, repetition—the same drive, in fact. "They
bring . . . They heel . . . They work . . .
They lift . . ." Again, the repetition underscores the
feeling the author has been creating from
the first paragraph—the awesome inevitability of
the events he is describing.

capelin eggs, and they will gorge as soon as the spawning starts.

Now, the most voracious of all the hunters appear. Fishing vessels come up over the horizon. They brought the Portuguese of the fifteenth century, who anchored offshore, dropped their boats, and rowed ashore to take the capelin with handnets, on beaches never before walked by white men. They brought Spaniards and Dutchmen, Englishmen and Irish, from the sixteenth to the twentieth centuries. Americans, Nova Scotians, Gloucestermen, schoonermen, bankermen, longliner captains have participated in the ritual. All of them knew that fresh capelin is the finest bait when it is skillfully used, and can attract a fortune in codfish flesh, hooked on the submarine banks to the south.

But presently, these hunters are Newfoundlanders. They bring their schooners flying inshore like great brown-and-white birds, a hundred, two hundred, three hundred sail. They heel through the screaming seabirds, luff, anchor, and drop their dories with the same precision of movement of the other figures in the ritual. In an hour, three thousand men are at work from the boats. They work as the codfish work, with a frenzy that knots forearms and sends nets spilling over the sterns to encircle the capelin. They lift a thousand tons of capelin out of the sea, yet they do not measurably diminish the number of fish.

Meanwhile, landbound hunters wait for the fish to come within range of their handnets. Women, children, and old people crowd the beach with the able-bodied men. The old people have ancestral memories of capelin bounty. In the seventeenth and eighteenth centuries, when food was often short, only the capelin harvest stood between them and starvation during the winter.

Many of the shore people are farmers who use the capelin for fertilizer as well as for food. Capelin corpses, spread to rot over thin northern soils, draw obedient crops of potatoes and cabbages out of the ground, and these, mixed with salted capelin flesh, become winter meals.

The children, who remember dried capelin as their candy, share the excitement of waiting. They chase one another up and down the beach and play with their own nets and fishing rods. Some are already asleep because they awoke before dawn to rouse the village, as they do every capelin morning with the cry: "They've a-come, they've a-come!"

Like the cod, the cunner, the flounder and the
sea birds, the people, too, seem predetermined to
attack the capelin as the little fish swarm
up on the beach. And once more, the author uses
the same device, repeated sentences beginning
with the word *they* to convey this to his reader.

Although the article is written in first person, the
pronoun *I* appears no more than a dozen
times. This is one of them. Yet, we feel the author's
presence in every line—all the more so,
perhaps, because he has wisely and modestly chosen
to stand aside and let the story itself prevail.

At the top of the beach, old women lie asleep or sit watching the seabirds squabbling and the dorymen rowing. They are Aunt Sadie and Little Nell and Bessie Blue and Mother Taunton, old ladies from several centuries. They know the capelin can save children in hard winters when the inshore cod fishery fails. They get up at two in the morning when the capelin are running, to walk miles to the nearest beach. They net a barrel of fish, then roll the barrel, which weighs perhaps a hundred pounds, back home. They have finished spreading the fish on their gardens, or salting them, before the first of their grandchildren awakes.

They have clear memories of catching capelin in winter, when the sea freezes close inshore and the tide cracks the ice in places. Then millions of capelin, resting out the winter, rise in the cracks. An old woman with a good net can take tons of passive fish out of the water for as long as her strength lasts and for as far as her net reaches.

A cry rises from the beach: "Here they come!"

The ritual must be played out, according to habit. The dorymen and the seabirds, the rampaging cod and cunner cannot touch or turn the purpose of the capelin. At a moment, its genesis unknown, they start for the shore. From the top of some nearby cliffs I watch and marvel at the precision of their behavior. The capelin cease to be a great formless mass offshore. They split into groups that the Newfoundlanders call *wads*—rippling gray lines, five to fifty feet wide—and run for the shore like advancing infantry lines. One by one, they peel away from their surviving comrades and advance, thirty to forty wads at a time.

Each wad has its discipline. The fish prepare to mate. Each male capelin seeks a female, darting from one fish to another. When he finds one, he presses against her side. Another male, perhaps two, press against her other side. The males urge the female on toward the beach. Some are struck down by diving seabirds but others take their places. Cod dash among them and smash their formations; they re-form immediately. Cunner rise and rip at them; flounder dart beneath them toward the beach.

The first wad runs into beach wavelets, and a hundred nets hit the water together; a silver avalanche of fish spills out on the beach. In each breaking wavelet the capelin maintain their formations, two or three males pressed tightly against the female until they are all flung up on the beach. There to the whispering

While we have commented glowingly on the overall
style of this article and the author's evident
craftsmanship, we should also point out that few
articles should or could be written in this
manner. The style, the treatment are perfect here—
perfect both for the kind of story and the high-
quality market for which it was written. This, of
course, is the ultimate test of a successful
article and the key to successful non-fiction writing—
does the piece suit the market for which
it was intended?

The author, having remained discreetly in the
background throughout the story, returns
at the end. The article, then, begins and ends with
the author's observations and comments.
This device gives the piece a classical dramatic unity.

sound of tiny fins and tails vibrating, the female convulsively digs into the sand, which is still moving in the wake of the retreating wave. As she goes down, she extrudes up to fifty thousand eggs, and the males expel their milt.

The children shout; their bare feet fly over the spawning fish; the nets soar; sea boots grind down; the fish spill out; gulls run in the shallows under the children's feet; the flounder gorge. A codfish, two feet long, leaps out of the shallows and hits the beach. An old man scoops it up. The wads keep coming. The air is filled with birds. The dorymen shout and laugh.

The flood of eggs becomes visible. The sand glistens with them. They pile in driftlines that writhe back and forth in each wave. The female capelin wiggle into masses of eggs. The shallows are permeated with eggs. The capelin breathe eggs. Their mouths fill with eggs. Their stomachs are choked with eggs. The wads keep pouring onward, feeding the disaster on the beach.

Down come the boots and the nets, and the capelin die, mouths open, oozing eggs. The spawning is a fiasco. The tide has turned. Instead of spawning on the shore with the assurance of rising water behind them, each wad strikes ashore in retreating water. Millions are stranded but the wads keep coming.

In the background, diminished by the quantity of fish, other players gasp and pant at their nets. Barrels stack high on the beach. Horses whinny, driven hard up the bank at the back of the beach. Carts laden with barrels weave away. Carts bringing empty barrels bounce and roar down. The wads are still coming. Men use shovels to lift dead and dying fish from driftlines that are now two and three feet high. The easterly wind is freshening. The wavelets become waves. The capelin are flung up on the beach without a chance to spawn. They bounce and twist and the water flees beneath them.

It is twilight, then dark; torches now spot the beach, the offshore dories, and the schooners. The waves grow solidly and pile the capelin higher. The men shovel the heaps into pyramids, then reluctantly leave. Heavy rain blots out beach and sea.

I remain to watch the blow piling up the sea. At the lowest point of the tide, it is driving waves high up on the beach, rolling the sand, digging up the partially buried eggs, and carrying them out to sea. By dawn most of the eggs are gone. The capelin have disappeared. The seabirds, the schooners, the cod, flounder,

Another device often found in highly literary
non-fiction writing is the rhetorical question. In the
closing paragraphs, the author asks
several to emphasize the riddle, the mystery of the
phenomenon he has described.

The ending, subtle and beautifully understated,
echoes the air of the mysterious and
inevitable which ran throughout the story.

cunner, eels, whales have gone. Nothing remains except the marks of human feet, the cart tracks on the high part of the beach, the odd pyramid of dead fish. The feast is done.

The empty arena of the beach suggests a riddle. If the capelin were so perfectly adapted to spawn on a rising tide, to master the task of burying eggs in running sand between waves, to know when the tide was rising, why did they continue spawning after the tide turned? Was that, by the ancient rules of the ritual, intentional? If it was, then it indicated a lethal error of adaptation that did not jibe with the great numbers of capelin.

I wonder, then, if the weak died and the strong survived, but dismiss the notion after recalling the indiscriminate nature of all capelin deaths. There was no Darwinian selection for death of the stupid or the inexperienced. Men slaughtered billions, this year and last year and for three hundred years before, but the capelin never felt this pin-pricking on their colossal corporate bodies. Their spawning was a disaster for reasons well beyond the influence of men.

A nineteenth-century observer, after seeing a capelin-spawning, recorded his amazement at "the astonishing *prosperity* of the creatures, cast so wilfully away...." It was in the end, and indeed throughout the entire ritual, the sheer numbers of capelin that scored the memory. The *prosperity* of the capelin preceded the disaster but then, it seemed, created it. Prosperity was not beneficial or an assurance of survival. The meaning of the ritual was slowly growing into sense. Prosperity unhinges the capelin. Prosperity, abundance, success, drive them on. They become transformed and throw themselves forward blindly....

I turn from the beach, warm and secure, and take a blind step forward.

About the author

Naturalist Franklin Russell is a prolific writer whose articles have appeared in magazines like *Maclean's, Holiday* and *Horizon*. His books are considered as authoritative and well-written as any in the nature field.

Acknowledgments

The Famous Writers School is grateful to these writers, publishers and literary agents for permission to use the materials listed below:

Americana Annual, 1964: passages from "Kennedy, John Fitzgerald" by Frank Freidel, © 1964 by Americana Corporation.

Mary Baumeister: "The Survival of a Family" from *McCall's,* issue of February 1967, permission by the author.

William A.H. Birnie: passages from "How to Write Magazine Articles" from *How to Write for Pleasure and Profit,* © 1951 by J.B. Lippincott Co.

Marchette Chute: passages from "America's Finest Library" from *Holiday,* March 1958.

Doubleday & Co., Inc.: passages from: *Never Call Retreat* by Bruce Catton, © 1965 by the author; *The Writer and His Markets* by Paul R. Reynolds, © 1959.

Wilfred Funk, Inc.: passages from: *Non-fiction: from Idea to Published Book* by Harry Edward Neal, © 1964; *Writing and Selling Fact and Fiction* by Harry Edward Neal, © 1949 by the author.

Gas Magazines, Inc.: "On Top of a Trend: The Pancake Inn" from *Cooking for Profit,* October 1965.

Geyer-McAllister Publications: passages from: "In-Store Convenience Attracts Drop-Ins" from *Geyer's Dealer Topics,* August 1965; "Selecting Good Outside Salesmen" by Frank Hanifin from *Geyer's Dealer Topics,* August 1965.

Good Housekeeping: "Rotary Power Mowers," reprinted by permission from *Good Housekeeping* magazine, July 1966, © 1966 by the Hearst Corp.

Harper & Row: passages from: *How to Write and Sell Magazine Articles* by Richard Gehman, © 1959 by the author; *How to Write, Speak and Think More Effectively* by Rudolf Flesch, © 1960 by the author; *Life of Sir Arthur Conan Doyle* by John Dickson Carr, © 1949 by the author; *Modern Feature Writing* by DeWitt C. Reddick, © 1949; *Tested Advertising Methods* by John Caples, © 1947 by the author; *Why Johnny Can't Read* by Rudolf Flesch, © 1955.

Dorothy H. Jenkins: "The Lure of Roses," © 1968 by Fawcett Publications, Inc. Appeared originally in *Woman's Day*. Reprinted by permission of *Woman's Day* magazine and McIntosh and Otis, Inc.

Wingate M. Johnson, M.D.: "Insomnia Can't Hurt You," © 1957 by the author and United Newspapers Magazine Corp., reprinted by permission of *This Week* magazine.

The Macmillan Co.: passages from *Magazine Article Writing* by Ernest Brennecke, Jr. and Donald Lemen Clark, © 1946.

John Thomas Mahoney: "New York to France in a Rowboat," as printed in *Coronet* magazine, permission of the author.

W.W. Norton & Co., Inc.: passages from *Spare-time Article Writing for Money* by W.J. Lederer, © 1954 by the author.

Popular Science Monthly: passages from "Booster Pump Gives New Life to Failing Hearts," December 1965.

Reader's Digest: "Antwerp's Glitter Street: World Diamond Center" by J.D. Ratcliff, January 1958; "Do Your Children Run Your Home?" by Sidonie Matsner Gruenberg with Llewellyn Miller, July 1959; "The Impossible Race from Peking to Paris" by J.D. Ratcliff, January 1958; "Interview With an Immortal" by Arthur Gordon, July 1959; "The Light in the Window" by Lois Mattox Miller, July 1959; "Our Amazing 'White Blood Stream' " by J.D. Ratcliff, January 1965; "Standing-up Country" by Paul and Myriam Friggens, May 1966; "The Wonder of the Winds" by J.D. Ratcliff, November 1965; "Your Amazing Circulatory System" by J.D. Ratcliff, January 1957.

Charles and Bonnie Remsberg: "What Went Wrong in Dreamland," reprinted by permission from the February 1967 issue of *Good Housekeeping* magazine, © 1967 by the Hearst Corp.

Rinehart & Co., Inc.: passages from *Article Writing and Marketing* by George L. Bird, © 1948 by the author.

The Ronald Press Company: passages from *How to Write and Sell Non-Fiction* by Hal Borland, © 1956 by the author.

Franklin Russell: "A Madness of Nature," reprinted by permission of John Cushman Associates, Inc., © 1968 by Franklin Russell.

Paul Schubert: passages from "Man Trackers of the Rockies" from the *Saturday Evening Post,* September 14, 1957.

Charles Scribner's Sons: passages from *A Guide to Successful Magazine Writing* by Morton Sontheimer, © 1954 by Charles Scribner's Sons. Reprinted by permission of Morton Sontheimer.

Science Service, Inc.: "Sea Food Exhaustible" from *Science News,* August 6, 1966.

Evelyn Singer: "Are Rich Widows Taking over the Country?" by Harold Mehling, © 1959 by the author and United Newspapers Magazine Corp., reprinted by permission of *This Week* magazine.

U.S. Lady: "The Wonder of the Winds" by J.D. Ratcliff, issue of October 1965.

John Wiley & Sons: passages from *Effective Writing* by H.J. Tichy, © 1966.

Willis Kingsley Wing: passages from "R.M.S. Titanic" by Hanson W. Baldwin, © 1934 by the author.

The Writer, Inc.: *Writing and Selling Magazine Articles* by Omer Henry, © 1962; "Self-Helps May Be Your Gold Mine" by Jean Z. Owen, *The Writer,* August 1958.

Writer's Digest: "The Do-It-Yourself Field" by V. Lee Oertle, © January 1957.

For permission to reproduce the pictures in Volume III and Volume IV, we thank the following:

Volume III

Robert C. Baxter: page 33; The Bettmann Archive, Inc.: page 63; Black Star Publishing Co., Inc.: Lennart Nilsson, page 131, W. Sanders, page 171, Louis Taeger, pages 9, 107; Brown Brothers: page 46; *Collier's* magazine, copyright Crowell Collier and Macmillan, Inc.: Robert Fawcett, page 51; Famous Schools Photo Department: pages 67, 110, 137, 149, 162; Free Lance Photographers Guild, Inc.: Arthur J. Lang, page 220; Hawthorne Books, Inc., *Treasury of Early American Homes:* page 23; Geo. A. Hormel & Co.: page 94; Library of Congress: pages 76, 113; *Look* magazine, copyright © 1965, Cowles Communications, Inc.: Bernie Fuchs, page 39; National Lead Company: page 28; *New York Daily News:* page 18; New York Public Library: page 73; Pan American Airways: page 30; Ernst Peterson: page 143; Pix, Inc.: Albert C. Flores, page 157, Tom Kelly, page 232; Province of Quebec Film Bureau: page 128; Rapho Guillumette Pictures: Laurence Lowry, page 176; Time, Inc., *Life,* June 20, 1967: page 5; U.S. Navy: PH1 Thomas Parkinson, page 15; Wide World Photos, Inc.: pages 80, 90, 104, 117, 134, 164.

Volume IV

The Bettmann Archive, Inc.: pages 375, 439; Black Star Publishing Co., Inc.: pages 254, 456, Gene Daniels, page 480, Dave Lawlor, page 466; Brown Brothers: page 309; Maury Delman: page 380; E.P. Dutton & Co., Inc.: page 378; Famous Schools Photo Department: pages 290, 295, 319, 351, 360, 363, 385, 388, 407, 417, 419, 422, 427, 444, 451, 459, 463; Free Lance Photographers Guild, Inc.: page 273, R.I. Nesmith, page 332, Ruth Sondak, page 316; Melvin Goldman: page 397; Maimonides Hospital, Brooklyn, N.Y.: page 327; New York Public Library: page 448; Province of Quebec Film Bureau: page 270; Rapho Guillumette Pictures: Esther Henderson, page 453, Ted Spiegel, page 335; *This Week* magazine and American Korean Foundation, Inc.: page 354; Otto Ulbrich Company, Inc.: pages 410, 411; United Press International, Inc.: pages 266, 284, 299, 329, 383, 391, 441; Wide World Photos, Inc.: pages 281, 341, 424, 435.

Index

A

These volumes are set in
Times New Roman type face,
used by the Famous Writers School
in all its publications.
The face was evolved for the
Times of London in 1932,
and is considered one of the most
readable of contemporary types.
Designed by Stanley Morison,
the eminent typographer and
printing historian,
it is a modernization of
earlier classic English designs.

Composed by Lettick Typografic, Inc.,
of Bridgeport, these volumes are
printed by Pace Litho of New York City.

They are bound by Russell-Rutter
Company, Inc., New York City.

The text paper is manufactured by
Fitchburg Paper Company
of Fitchburg, Massachusetts.

The format and binding are designed
by Bradbury Thompson.